WINNERS ARE NOT THOSE WHO NEVER FAIL BUT THOSE W

NEVER QUIT

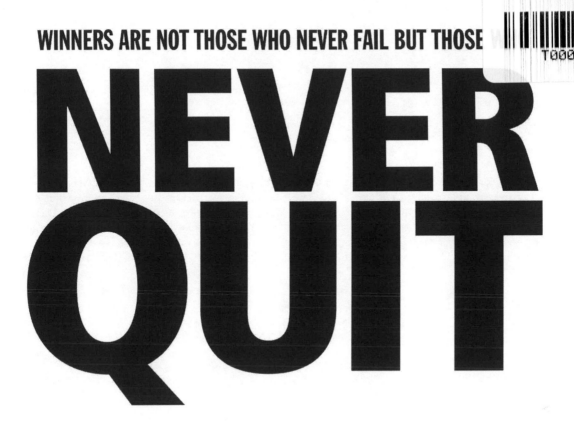

MAJORING IN MEN®
The Curriculum for Men

Edwin Louis Cole

WHITAKER
HOUSE

NEVER QUIT WORKBOOK

Christian Men's Network
P.O. Box 3
Grapevine, TX 76099
www.ChristianMensNetwork.com

Facebook.com/EdwinLouisCole

ISBN: 979-8-88769-146-6
Printed in the United States of America
© 2014 Edwin and Nancy Cole Legacy LLC

Published by:
Whitaker House
1030 Hunt Valley Circle
New Kensington, PA 15068

TABLE OF CONTENTS

Lesson 1

God Will Make a Way
&
God Will Be Faithful to You

Lesson 1
God Will Make a Way & God Will Be Faithful to You

I. God Will Make a Way (Chapter 1)

    A. Fill in the statements below with the following words: *(pages 9-10)*

        success   outcome   normal   crisis   part

        1. _____ is generally the reason behind feelings of wanting to give up.

        2. Facing the crisis can lead to our greatest _____.

        3. Change and crisis are _____ to life.

        4. The _____ rests not in the nature of the issue but in what we do with the crisis.

        5. We do our _____.

    B. Crisis is common in life. *(page 11)*   ____ True   ____ False

        1. Christians should not experience crisis. *(page 11)*   ____ True   ____ False
            Read 2 Corinthians 11:23-29.

For Further Study:

Change produces crisis. Change is normal, so crisis is normal to life – *"In the world ye shall have tribulation"* John 16:33. Crisis has sorrow in it, but sorrow is life's greatest teacher – Ecclesiastes 7:3; *"It is good for me that I have been afflicted; that I might learn thy statutes"* Psalm 119:71.

All true joy is born out of sorrow – *"Weeping may endure for a night, but joy cometh in the morning … Thou hast turned for me my mourning into dancing: thou hast put off my sackcloth, and girded me with gladness"* Psalm 30:5, 11; *"They that sow in tears shall reap in joy"* Psalm 126:5.

God wants every change in the lives of His children to be good – Romans 8:28. Let God take you through each crisis to the next stage of life – Romans 8:38, 39.

Always remember that God is for you, not against you – Psalm 56:9.

Be careful not to waste your youth brooding over what someone else has done to you – Isaiah 43:14, 18.

2. What is the factor that makes a crisis seem so unbearable? *(page 11)* _____

3. Stress is a modern phenomenon that should be avoided at all costs. *(page 11)*

    ____ True   ____ False

C. What can you learn from Apostle Paul's ordeal with a ship captain's poor decision? *(pages 13-14)*

    _____

II. God Will Be Faithful to You (Chapter Two)

A. Read: *"Know therefore that the Lord thy God, He is God, the faithful God, which keepeth covenant and mercy with them that love him and keep His commandments to a thousand generations"* Deuteronomy 7:9.
    Circle the words that assure you that God can be trusted with your life.

B. What are believers really saying when they ask, "If God exists, why does He allow wars, birth defects, disease, etc."? *(page 18)*

    _____

    _____

For Further Study:

Apostle Paul's crises were many and varied – *"Are they ministers of Christ? ... I am more; in labours more abundant, in stripes above measure, in prisons more frequent, in deaths oft. Of the Jews five times received I forty stripes save one. Thrice was I beaten with rods, once was I stoned, thrice I suffered shipwreck, a night and a day I have been in the deep; In journeyings often, in perils of waters, in perils of robbers, in perils by mine own countrymen, in perils by the heathen, in perils in the city, in perils in the wilderness, in perils in the sea, in perils among false brethren; In weariness and painfulness, in watchings often, in hunger and thirst, in fastings often, in cold and nakedness. Beside those things that are without, that which cometh upon me daily, the care of all the churches. Who is weak, and I am not weak? who is offended, and I burn not?"* 2 Corinthians 11:23-29.
Apostle Paul's ordeal with the ship's captain – Acts 27:9-44

1. When believers ask, "Will God work," are they asking if God is powerful enough to do it? *(page 18)* ____ Yes ____ No

    What are they really asking? *(page 18)* _____

2. Men hardly ever doubt God's ability, but they do doubt His _____. *(page 18)*

3. The victory of the redeemed is not that they transform the world, but _____

    _____

    _____

    _____. *(page 19)*

C. Read aloud 2 Timothy 2:2.

    1. Talent cannot compensate for a lack of _____. *(page 19)*

    2. Faithful men are the _____ of the Church. *(page 20)*

    Read aloud 1 Corinthians 4:2.

    Define "faithfulness." *(page 20)* _____

    _____

For Further Study:

God is faithful! – *"Know therefore that the Lord thy God, he is God, the faithful God, which keepeth covenant and mercy with them that love him and keep his commandments to a thousand generations"* Deuteronomy 7:9. Faith in God honors Him; unbelief dishonors Him – *"But without faith it is impossible to please him: for he that cometh to God must believe that he is, and that he is a rewarder of them that diligently seek him"* Hebrews 11:6. God's Word is the source of faith – *"Man shall not live by bread alone, but by every word that proceedeth out of the mouth of God"* Matthew 4:4.

D. Faithfulness is a mark of _____. *(page 21)*

    1. List the evidences of faithfulness. *(page 21)*

        a. _____   b. _____   c. _____

    2. God is faithful toward some when He feels like it. *(pages 21-22)*   ____ True   ____ False

E. Read Hebrews 1:3. With what does God uphold the world? *(page 22)*

    _____

    1. God never varies. *(page 23)*   ____ True   ____ False
        Read James 1:17.

    2. What is the difference between worry and faith? *(page 25)*

    _____

    3. When we worry about ourselves, we are really worrying about God. *(page 25)*

    ____ True   ____ False

For Further Study:

Renew your mind – *"Lie not … seeing you have put off the old man … And have put on the new man"* Colossians 3:9, 10; *"And be not conformed to this world: but be ye transformed by the renewing of your mind, that ye may prove what is that good, and acceptable, and perfect will of God"* Romans 12:2.

God transforms our whole lives with His love – *"Therefore if any man be in Christ, he is a new creature: old things are passed away; behold, all things are become new"* 2 Corinthians 5:17; *"And hope maketh not ashamed; because the love of God is shed abroad in our hearts by the Holy Ghost which is given unto us"* Romans 5:5.

Heart change – *"Circumcision is that of the heart, in the spirit, and not in the letter"* Romans 2:29; *"A new heart also will I give you, and a new spirit will I put within you: and I will take away the stony heart out of your flesh, and I will give you an heart of flesh"* Ezekiel 36:26.

Faithfulness – *"And the things that thou hast heard of me among many witnesses, the same commit thou to faithful men, who shall be able to teach others also"* 2 Timothy 2:2.

4. When we worry about an outcome after we've prayed, what are we basically saying about God?

   (pages 25-26) _____

   _____

F. Read: *"Even when we are too weak to have any faith left, he remains faithful to us and will help us, for he cannot disown us who are part of himself, and he will always carry out his promises to us"* 2 Timothy 2:13 TLB.

   1. To make God the _____ for our failures is to _____ His

      ability to be the _____. *(page 29)*

   2. To accuse God of _____ is to accuse Him of not being God. *(page 30)*

   3. God takes what is meant for evil and turns it _____

      _____. *(page 32)*

For Further Study:

Lay a right foundation for your character – 2 Corinthians 7:1. Character is built in private. It develops out of a lifetime of individual decisions which either enhance or diminish it – *"I have chosen the way of truth: thy judgments have I laid before me"* Psalm 119:30; *"If a man therefore purge himself from these, he shall be a vessel unto honour, sanctified, and meet for the master's use, and prepared unto every good work"* 2 Timothy 2:21. Personality is not the same as character – Proverbs 26:23. Personality is after the outward man and is temporal – 1 Samuel 16:7.
Obedience to His Word honors God; disobedience dishonors Him – 1 Samuel 15:22, 23; Proverbs 14:2.
Creator God – *"Who being the brightness of his glory, and the express image of his person, and upholding all things by the word of his power, when he had by himself purged our sins, sat down on the right hand of the Majesty on high"* Hebrews 1:3; *"And he is before all things, and by him all things consist"* Colossians 1:17; *"Thou art worthy, O Lord, to receive glory and honour and power: for thou hast created all things, and for thy pleasure they are and were created"* Revelation 4:11.

Practical:

What has God spoken to your heart in studying just these first two chapters?

_____

_____

Repeat this prayer out loud:

Father, I never realized how much I haven't trusted You. I have blamed You, accused You, worried about You, but today I want to truly trust You. Please forgive my past, and let me start today anew. Amen.

For Further Study:

God never changes – James 1:17; *"God is not a man, that he should lie; neither the son of man, that he should repent: hath he said, and shall he not do it? or hath he spoken, and shall he not make it good?"* Numbers 23:19; *"For I am the Lord, I change not; therefore ye sons of Jacob are not consumed"* Malachi 3:6.

Pray – *"Don't worry about anything; instead pray about everything; tell God your needs and don't forget to thank him for his answers"* Philippians 4:6 TLB; *"It is a good thing to give thanks unto the Lord"* Psalm 92:1.

God cannot be unfaithful – *"If we believe not, yet he abideth faithful: he cannot deny himself"* 2 Timothy 2:13.

God's transcendent glory – *"But as for you, ye thought evil against me; but God meant it unto good, to bring to pass, as it is this day, to save much people alive"* Genesis 50:20.

God's Word is the source of faith – *"I have inclined mine heart to perform thy statutes always, even unto the end"* Psalm 119:112.

Self Test *Lesson 1*

1. Crisis is normal to life.

    ____ True   ____ False

2. Stress is never good for us.

    ____ True   ____ False

3. Men often doubt God's ability but never His faithfulness.

    ____ True   ____ False

4. What are three evidences of faithfulness in a man?

    a. _____   b. _____   c. _____

5. What is the main difference between worry and faith? _____

    _____

6. If we experience failure, God can and will disown us.   ____ True   ____ False

7. What is one way to eliminate God as the source of our solutions? _____

    _____

8. To accuse God of failure is to accuse Him of _____

    _____.

9. Failure can be the _____ of success.

10. God is faithful even when we are _____.

Keep this test for your own records.

Lesson 2

God Will Speak to You

Lesson 2
God Will Speak to You

A. Elijah was a man of _____ and _____. *(pages 35-36)*

    1. List three ways Elijah brought glory to God. *(page 36)*

       a. _____   c. _____

       b. _____

    2. Name the five-fold temptations common to crisis. *(page 36)*

       a. _____   c. _____   e. _____

       b. _____   d. _____

    3. Where did Elijah fight his toughest battle? *(page 37)* _____

    4. Once the battle is won, you have no worries. *(page 37)*   ____ True   ____ False

B. Read 1 Kings 18 & 19.

    1. What was the nature of this biblical confrontation? _____

    2. God hates those who say bad is good and good is bad. *(page 40)*   ____ True   ____ False

    3. Name three of Satan's tactics. Circle the one to which Elijah fell prey. *(page 43)*

       a. _____   b. _____   c. _____

For Further Study:

Elijah moved the arm of God in prayer – *"Elias was a man subject to like passions as we are, and he prayed earnestly that it might not rain: and it rained not on the earth by the space of three years and six months. And he prayed again, and the heaven gave rain, and the earth brought forth her fruit"* James 5:17-18; 1 Kings 17-19.
The Christian must know the truth, so he can recognize the lies of Satan and fight for the honor of God – Proverbs 2:6-9.
God's Word is the source of truth – John 17:7. God's Spirit guides into all truth – John 16:13.
Satan's mission – *"Your enemy the devil prowls around like a roaring lion looking for someone to devour"* 1 Peter 5:8 NIV.

4. When Elijah wanted to give up and give in, what was God's attitude? *(page 45)*

   _____

5. What three things did Elijah need for recovery? *(page 46)*

   a. _____   b. _____   c. _____

6. What did Elijah and Jesus both take time to do? *(page 46)*

   _____

C. Name the basic art of communication. *(page 47)* _____

   1. What did Elijah STOP doing before God spoke to him? *(circle one)* *(page 48)*

      a. waiting on the mount   b. sinning   c. feeling sorry for himself

   2. In quietness, Elijah heard from God and became ready to receive the revelation that would

      _____. *(page 48)*

   3. What is the "beauty" of the relationship between God and Elijah? *(page 48)*

      _____

D. Whether or not we experience a turning point in our lives when God reaches out to us depends on: *(circle one)* *(page 49)*

   a. our obedience to His Word   b. our Christian heritage   c. Him

   1. Rewrite the following sentence **in your own words:** *(page 49)*

      "God's power is released in our lives to the degree of our obedience and no more."

      _____

For Further Study:

God ministered to Elijah – *"And as he lay and slept under a juniper tree ... an angel touched him, and said unto him, Arise and eat ... And he did eat and drink, and laid him down again. And the angel of the Lord came again the second time, and touched him, and said, Arise and eat; because the journey is too great for thee. And he arose, and did eat and drink"* 1 Kings 19:5-8.

Reliable communication *"permits progress"* Proverbs 13:17 TLB; Mark 4:11-12, 23-24.

Distortion – *"When the crowd heard the voice, some of them thought it was thunder"* John 12:28-29 TLB; *"And they will deceive every one his neighbour, and will not speak the truth: they have taught their tongue to speak lies, and weary themselves to commit iniquity"* Jeremiah 9:5; Romans 16:18.

Getting away to pray – Matthew 14:23

God spoke to Elijah in a *"still small voice"* – 1 Kings 19:12-15.

2. Emotions follow _____. *(page 49)*

3. What does "righteousness" mean? *(page 49)* _____

4. How can you change your emotions? *(page 50)* _____

5. How can someone "see" faith? *(page 50)* _____

6. What is God's method of protection? *(page 50)* _____

E. What is the hardest thing in the world for a man to take? *(circle one)* *(page 51)*

a. rejection   b. loss of a business   c. divorce

1. Read aloud: *"For He [God] Himself has said, I will not in any way fail you nor give you up nor leave you without support. [I will] not, [I will] not, [I will] not in any degree leave you helpless nor forsake nor let [you] down (relax My hold on you)! [Assuredly not!] So we take comfort and are encouraged and confidently and boldly say, The Lord is my Helper; I will not be seized with alarm [I will not fear or dread or be terrified]. What can man do to me?"* Hebrews 13:5b-6 AMP.

2. Will God ever stop working for your good? *(page 51)*   ____ Yes   ____ No

3. God brings you _____ in order to take you _____. *(page 51)*

4. _____ is the only means of exchange. *(page 51)*

___

For Further Study:

Our actions confirm our words and determine our emotions – Psalm 126:5; Matthew 15:18; Luke 6:45; 2 Corinthians 7:1; 2 Timothy 2:21; *"And let us not be weary in well doing: for in due season we shall reap, if we faint not"* Galatians 6:9.

Righteousness – Romans 3:22, 25-26; 4:3, 5; 5:18-19

The result of faith – James 2:17-18, 20, 22

God's promises are conditional – *"If ye be willing and obedient, ye shall eat the good of the land"* Isaiah 1:19.

God desires our highest good – *"Being confident of this very thing, that he which hath begun a good work in you will perform it until the day of Jesus Christ"* Philippians 1:6.

F. What is God's simple command to husbands? *(page 52)*

_____

1. Love is the desire to benefit _____ even at the expense of _____ because love

    desires to _____. *(page 53)*

2. It is prideful to think that God works on my behalf. *(page 54)*   ____ True   ____ False

Practical:

1. Satan uses three tatics against you. Which was the last one that got to you? What do you know now
    that can help you change the outcome?

    _____

    _____

2. Think of men you know who sit under a juniper tree in their jobs, marriages or with their children,
    yet nothing changes. If God gave you the opportunity, what could you tell those men today?

    _____

    _____

Repeat this prayer out loud:

*Father God, I want out from under the juniper tree—permanently! Help me understand and believe that truly You
are working for my highest good. Forgive me of disobedience, and help me to obey. When I'm tempted, please bring
to my mind that obedience is for my benefit. In Jesus' Name. Amen.*

For Further Study:

Love and submission are for everyone – *"Submitting yourselves one to another in the fear of God. Wives, submit
yourselves unto your own husbands, as unto the Lord … Husbands, love your wives, even as Christ also loved the
church, and gave himself for it … So ought men to love their wives as their own bodies. He that loveth his wife
loveth himself. For no man every yet hated his own flesh; but nourisheth and cherisheth it, even as the Lord the
church … Nevertheless let every one of you in particular so love his wife even as himself; and the wife see that she
reverence her husband"* Ephesians 5:21, 22, 25, 28, 29, 33.

God's love – *"But God commendeth his love toward us, in that, while we were yet sinners, Christ died for us …
For if, when we were enemies, we were reconciled to God by the death of his Son, much more, being reconciled,
we shall be saved by his life"* Romans 5:8, 10; *"Fear not, little flock; for it is your Father's good pleasure to give
you the kingdom"* Luke 12:32; 2 Peter 1:3.

Self Test *Lesson 2*

1. What are the five-fold temptations common to crisis?

    a. _____   d. _____

    b. _____   e. _____

    c. _____

2. Where did Elijah fight his toughest battle? _____

3. The day before the battle is always more important than the day after.   ____ True   ____ False

4. Elijah was a supernatural man, unlike men today.   ____ True   ____ False

5. If Satan cannot gain an advantage by _____, he will try to defeat by

    _____. If neither of those work, he'll try _____.

6. God gave up on Elijah when Elijah had given up on himself.   ____ True   ____ False

7. What three things did God do for Elijah to bring him recovery?

    a. _____

    b. _____

    c. _____

8. God waited until Elijah was _____ before He spoke.

9. What is the basic art of communication? _____

10. God's power is released in our lives to the degree of _____.

11. What is God's method of protection for us? _____

Keep this test for your own records.

Lesson 3
God Will Restore All

Lesson 3
God Will Restore All

A. What determines a man's destiny? *(page 56)* _____

   1. When David compromised his position, who was also compromised? *(page 56)*

   _____

   2. When David's decision took him away from God's will, it took him out of God's reach. *(page 57)*

   ____ True   ____ False

   3. What was David's response when Ziklag was plundered? *(page 57)* _____

   4. How did David encourage himself? *(page 58)* _____

   _____

   _____

   5. What is prayerlessness really, oftentimes? *(page 58)* _____

   6. Read 1 Samuel 30.

For Further Study:

It takes courage to make decisions – *"Choose you this day whom ye will serve ... but as for me and my house, we will serve the Lord"* Joshua 24:15.

A man who has learned to honor God privately will show good character in his decisions publicly – *"I have refrained my feet from every evil way, that I might keep thy word. I have not departed from thy judgments: for thou hast taught me ... Through thy precepts I get understanding: therefore I hate every false way"* Psalm 119:101, 102, 104.

Decision translates into energy – *"A double minded man is unstable in all his ways"* James 1:8.

Decision motivates to action – Example: Solomon – *"And Solomon determined to build an house for the name of the Lord"* 2 Chronicles 2:1; Write down your decision so you'll be motivated to hold to it – *"Write the vision, and make it plain upon tables, that he may run that readeth it"* Habakkuk 2:2.

7. When David recovered spiritually, what else did he recover? *(page 58)*

_____

B. How did David almost lose it all? *(page 59)* _____

1. _____ is the basis for sin. *(page 59)*

2. Name some of the things men miss through impatience. *(page 60)*

a. _____

b. _____

c. _____

C. What strange thing can believers do in the face of crisis? *(page 60)* _____

1. Why can they do that? *(page 60)* _____

2. Read Acts 16:25-26. Explain how Paul and Silas probably felt.

_____

_____

3. What heartfelt understanding kept Paul from fearing evil? *(page 61)*

_____

4. The purposes of God will be served by God Himself. *(page 61)* ____ True ____ False

---

For Further Study:

Be encouraged by what you write down – *"And David was greatly distressed; for the people spake of stoning him, because the soul of all the people was grieved, every man for his sons and for his daughters: but David encouraged himself in the Lord his God"* 1 Samuel 30:6.

Recovering all – *"And David recovered all that the Amalekites had carried away"* 1 Samuel 30:18.

All sin is deceitful – *"But exhort one another daily, while it is called Today; lest any of you be hardened through the deceitfulness of sin"* Hebrews 3:13.

Five sins that keep us out of a personal "Land of Promise" – Exodus 32:1-10; 19-35; Numbers 14; 25:1-9; Romans 1:18-32; 1 Corinthians 6:9-10; Hebrews 3:7-19; Jude 7; Revelation 22:15

D. What is the best evidence Christians have that God will work for our highest good? *(page 62)*

_____

_____

1. Write out Romans 8:32.

_____

_____

2. Read 1 Corinthians 10:13. Rephrase this **in your own words.**

_____

_____

3. God will disown you when you are going through horrific circumstances or are in the midst of temptations. *(page 62)* _____ True _____ False

4. In the moment of your need, your trust must be _____. *(page 63)*

E. Name biblical characters God was faithful to. _____

Name biblical characters God was <u>un</u>faithful to. _____

For Further Study:

Prodigal son – *"Father, give me the portion of goods that falleth to me ... And [he] took his journey into a far country, and there wasted his substance with riotous living. And when he had spent all, there arose a mighty famine in that land ... And he would fain have filled his belly with the husks that the swine did eat ... And when he came to himself, he said, How many hired servants of my father's have bread enough and to spare, and I perish with hunger! ... And he arose, and came to his father ... Father, I have sinned against heaven, and in thy sight, and am no more worthy to be called thy son. But the father said to his servants ... this my son was dead, and is alive again; he was lost, and is found. And they began to be merry"* Luke 15:11-24.

Praise the Lord – *"Rejoice in the Lord, O ye righteous: for praise is comely for the upright"* Psalm 33:1; *"And at midnight Paul and Silas prayed, and sang praises unto God: and the prisoners heard them. And suddenly there was a great earthquake, so that the foundations of the prison were shaken: and immediately all the doors were opened, and every one's bands were loosed"* Acts 16:25-26.

Practical:

1. What are areas of impatience in your life?

    _____

    _____

2. What do you think you may have missed out on through impatience?

    _____

    _____

3. What can you do TODAY to change that?

    _____

    _____

4. Meditate on: *"For He [God] Himself has said, I will not in any way fail you nor give you up nor leave you without support. [I will] not, [I will] not, [I will] not in any degree leave you helpless nor forsake nor let [you] down (relax My hold on you)! [Assuredly not!]"* Hebrews 13:5b AMP.

Repeat this prayer out loud:

Father, in the Name of Jesus, I come to You right now. In the midst of my need, I want to be honest with You. I don't have to feel anything, sense anything, generate anything. I just want You to know that I believe You are my God. I believe Your Word is true. I believe that, right now, You are working for my highest good. Thank You for not denying me, because You will not deny Yourself. I trust You totally to bring me into a new revelation, greater ministry and greater blessing than I have ever known in my life. Amen.

For Further Study:

God is faithful – *"There hath no temptation taken you but such as is common to man: but God is faithful, who will not suffer you to be tempted above that ye are able; but will with the temptation also make a way to escape, that ye may be able to bear it"* 1 Corinthians 10:13.

Basic temptations – *"For all that is in the world, the lust of the flesh, and the lust of the eyes, and the pride of life, is not of the Father, but is of the world"* 1 John 2:16.

Self Test *Lesson 3*

1. Decisions determine _____.

2. Prayerlessness is often a form of _____.

3. What is the one thing that causes most people to miss what God has for them?

   _____

4. God, in His wrath, will disown us as His children in the midst of our suffering and trials.

   ____ True   ____ False

5. What is one of the strongest weapons we can employ during trials and temptations?

   _____

6. When David's city of Ziklag was plundered, what was his response?

   _____

7. Your sins and mistakes can take you out of the reach of God's help.

   ____ True   ____ False

8. Before David could recover all that was lost materially in the plundering of Ziklag, he had to recover

   _____.

Keep this test for your own records.

Lesson 4

God's Pattern for Change

Lesson 4
God's Pattern for Change

A.   Everything God does is according to a _____ and based on a _____. *(page 67)*

    1.   How can our lives become productive, maximized and successful? *(page 67)* _____

    _____

    2.   What are the two things we do in life? *(page 68)*

       a. _____   b. _____

    3.   Change accompanies _____. *(page 68)*

B.   What is the corresponding principle to the pattern of "entering and leaving"? *(page 69)*

_____

For Further Study:

It is God's desire for His Church to know His patterns and principles – *"The secret things belong unto the Lord our God: but those things which are revealed belong unto us and to our children for ever, that we may do all the words of this law"* Deuteronomy 29:29.

Pattern for Increase		Pattern for Failure	
Identification	– Acts 2:42, 43	Deception	– Genesis 3:4, 5
Involvement	– Acts 2:44	Distraction	– Genesis 3:6
Investment	– Acts 2:45	Dislocation	– Genesis 3:7-10
Increase	– Acts 2:46-47	Destruction	– Genesis 3:23

1. What is left in our mind and spirit from the old determines: *(page 69)*

   _____

2. Seeds we carry for good will produce what? *(page 69)* _____

3. What do seeds of righteousness produce? *(page 71)* _____

4. God doesn't care about root causes, just external actions. *(page 71)*

   ____ True   ____ False

5. How we _____ determines how we _____. *(page 71)*

C. God's escape pattern is never based on an escape _____, but an escape _____. *(page 71)*

   1. Write out Deuteronomy 6:23. _____

      _____

      _____

For Further Study:

How you leave determines how you enter – *"Be not deceived; God is not mocked: for whatsoever a man soweth, that shall he also reap"* Galatians 6:7.

How you leave one sphere or experience of life will determine how you enter the next – 2 Peter 1:10, 11.

Learn to take advantage of the crises in your life. Use them to bring you closer to God – *"For I am persuaded, that neither death, nor life, nor angels, nor principalities, nor powers, nor things present, nor things to come, Nor height, nor depth, nor any other creature, shall be able to separate us from the love of God, which is in Christ Jesus our Lord"* Romans 8:38, 39.

2. God always thinks in terms of _____ us to something better. *(page 72)*

3. What was the mental attitude that kept Israel from inhabiting Canaan? *(page 73)*

    _____

4. What is God's primary, fundamental goal for our lives? *(page 74)*

    _____

5. To bring us into Christlikeness, what does God have to bring us out of? *(page 74)*

    _____

6. What happens as we enter the new and leave the old? *(page 74)*

    _____

D. God is more concerned with _____

    than _____. *(page 75)*

    1. God always looks at: *(circle one) (page 75)*
        a. the sin   b. our perspective   c. the finished product

For Further Study:

How to build great works – *"A good man out of the good treasure of his heart bringeth forth that which is good"* Luke 6:45; Hebrews 1:3; 11:3; *"Let no corrupt communication proceed out of your mouth, but that which is good to the use of edifying, that it may minister grace unto the hearers"* Ephesians 4:29; *"Who is a wise man and endued with knowledge among you? let him show out of a good conversation his works with meekness of wisdom"* James 3:13.

2. Fill in the statements with these words: *(page 77)*
   entering   leaving

   a. _____ is necessary to _____.

   b. _____ is as important as _____.

E. Write "T" for True and "F" for False statements below: *(pages 78-81)*

_____ 1. If we look for God only in the spectacular, we will miss the Holy Spirit.

_____ 2. Money is the essential ingredient in success.

_____ 3. You can never stay too long, once God puts you there.

_____ 4. Success comes when you are the right man, at the right time, in the right place.

_____ 5. At "Kadesh Barnea," we need to say, "No more! What shall I learn here?"

_____ 6. Nothing will ever erase the failures of your past.

_____ 7. It shows little humility when you say God wants you to go from "glory to glory."

_____ 8. The pattern you used in one business may not work for the next.

For Further Study:
God brings you out in order to take you in – *"And he brought us out from thence, that he might bring us in, to give us the land which he sware unto our fathers"* Deuteronomy 6:23; Numbers 13-14.

F.   List the pattern for the harvest. *(page 81)*

1. _____   3. _____

2. _____   4. _____

Practical:

1.   What are some ways the "pattern for harvest" could be applied in your life?

_____

_____

2.   What are some areas in which you've had the attitude of wanting to "escape"? What can you do instead?

_____

_____

For Further Study:

Receive God's power in your life – *"But now I go my way to him that sent me; and none of you asketh me, Whither goest thou? But because I have said these things unto you, sorrow hath filled your heart. Nevertheless I tell you the truth; It is expedient for you that I go away: for if I go not away, the Comforter will not come unto you; but if I depart, I will send him unto you"* John 16:5-7; *"But ye shall receive power, after that the Holy Ghost is come upon you: and ye shall be witnesses unto me both in Jerusalem, and in all Judaea, and in Samaria, and unto the uttermost part of the earth"* Acts 1:8.

3. Read: *"Looking away [from all that will distract] to Jesus, Who is the Leader and the Source of our faith [giving the first incentive for our belief] and is also its Finisher [bringing it to maturity and perfection]. He, for the joy [of obtaining the prize] that was set before Him, endured the cross, despising and ignoring the shame, and is now seated at the right hand of the throne of God. Just think of Him Who endured from sinners such grievous opposition and bitter hostility against Himself [reckon up and consider it all in comparison with your trials], so that you may not grow weary or exhausted, losing heart and relaxing and fainting in your minds"* Hebrews 12:2-3 AMP.

Repeat this prayer out loud:

Father, in Jesus' Name, help me understand the difference between my desire to escape a situation and Your desire to bring me into another situation. Please forgive me for the bad seeds I've carried forward into my present from my past. Help me to correct that wrong now, in Jesus' Name. I will work the pattern of the harvest, for Your glory in my life. Let it be so, Amen.

For Further Study:

Make changes – *"Plant the good seeds of righteousness and you will reap a crop of my love; plow the hard ground of your hearts, for now is the time to seek the Lord, that he may come and shower salvation upon you"* Hosea 10:12 TLB; *"Today if you will hear his voice, Harden not your hearts"* Hebrews 3:7-8; *"If you are angry, don't sin by nursing your grudge. Don't let the sun go down with you still angry — get over it quickly. For when you are angry you give a mighty foothold to the devil"* Ephesians 4:26 TLB.
Persevere to mature – *"Never tire of doing what is right"* 2 Thessalonians 3:13; Matthew 5:48 AMP; Romans 5:3-5 NIV; 8:37; 1 Corinthians 15:58; 1 Timothy 4:16; Hebrews 3:6; 6:1 TLB; 12:1-3.
Never quit – *"No, dear brothers, I am still not all I should be but I am bringing all my energies to bear on this one thing: Forgetting the past and looking forward to what lies ahead, I strain to reach the end of the race and receive the prize for which God is calling us up to heaven because of what Christ Jesus did for us"* Philippians 3:13, 14 TLB.

Self Test *Lesson 4*

1. God does everything according to a _____ and based upon a _____.

2. Describe the pattern of entering and leaving.

   _____

3. What always comes with change? _____

4. God's escape pattern is never based on an escape *to* but an escape *from*.   ____ True   ____ False

5. God always thinks in terms of _____ us to something better.

6. What is God's primary, fundamental goal for our lives?

   _____

7. You leave the old and enter the new by way of _____.

8. God is more concerned with where we have come from, than where we are going.

   ____ True   ____ False

9. If God brings you into something supernaturally, it's always important that you stay there.

   ____ True   ____ False

10. The essential ingredient in success is _____.

11. List the pattern of the harvest.

    a. _____

    b. _____

    c. _____

    d. _____

Keep this test for your own records.

Lesson 5

Steps to Entering and Leaving
(Part One)

Lesson 5
Steps to Entering and Leaving (Part One)

A. _____ is normal to life. *(page 83)*

   While in transition, where you are is not as important as _____. *(page 84)*

   While God changes where you are, He will also change what? *(page 84)*

   _____

B. Jesus' forgiveness opened _____ to us. *(page 85)*

   1. Read John 20:23.

   2. Forgiveness _____, unforgiveness _____. *(page 85)*

   3. List things that are shut down through unforgiveness. *(page 86)*

   _____

   4. List ways you can think of that can communicate unforgiveness. *(pages 86-87)*

   _____

For Further Study:

The principal of release states that only after sins are released are people free to become what God wants them to be – Matthew 6:14, 15.

The sins you forgive are released, and the sins you do not forgive are retained in your life. In order to activate this principle in your life, admit the Holy Spirit into your heart and be guided and directed by Him – *"And having said this, He breathed on them and said to them, Receive the Holy Spirit! [Now having received the Holy Spirit, and being led and directed by Him] if you forgive the sins of anyone, they are forgiven; if you retain the sins of anyone, they are retained"* John 20:22-23 AMP.

Healing takes place when, by faith, the principle of release is acted upon – Hebrews 12:1.

5. When you do not forgive, what valuable thing is closed off to others? *(page 87)*

    _____

6. Can forgiveness be earned? *(page 87)*   ____ Yes   ____ No

7. When you leave one situation or place for another, what do you take with you? *(page 87)*

    _____

8. What shouldn't you take with you? *(page 87)*

    _____

C. Admit that _____ is your source. *(page 88)*

    1. Read Proverbs 3:9.

    2. Write out Hebrews 13:6. _____

        _____

        _____

    3. Where are our financial battles won? *(circle one)* *(page 90)*

        a. on our knees   b. at the bank   c. just with good money management

For Further Study:

Grace – *"In whom we have redemption through his blood, the forgiveness of sins, according to the riches of his grace"* Ephesians 1:7; *"For by grace are ye saved through faith; and that not of yourselves: it is the gift of God"* Ephesians 2:8; *"Not by works of righteousness which we have done, but according to his mercy he saved us, by the washing of regeneration, and renewing of the Holy Ghost"* Titus 3:5.

God will help you – *"So that we may boldly say, The Lord is my helper, and I will not fear what man shall do unto me"* Hebrews 13:6.

Financial health based on faith – *"He which soweth sparingly shall reap also sparingly; and he which soweth bountifully shall reap also bountifully"* 2 Corinthians 9:6; James 2:17-20.

4. Never stop honoring God with your _____. *(page 90)*

5. You cannot compensate by sacrifice _____

    _____. *(page 90)*

6. Expecting God to instantaneously release us from a lifetime of error is _____,

    not _____ . *(page 91)*

7. What causes life's disappointments? *(page 91)* _____

    _____

8. God honors those who _____. *(page 91)*

    Read 1 Samuel 2:30.

9. What is the relationship between forgiveness and giving? *(page 92)*

    _____

10. What will reverence for God get you? *(page 92)*

    _____

For Further Study:

Jesus cares how people use money – Mark 12:41; *"Jesus said unto him, If thou wilt be perfect, go and sell that thou hast, and give to the poor, and thou shalt have treasure in heaven: and come and follow me"* Matthew 19:21; Luke 19:8; Acts 5:1-2.

Covetous v. Generous – *"It is possible to give away and become richer! It is also possible to hold on too tightly and lose everything. Yes, the liberal man shall be rich! By watering others, he waters himself"* Proverbs 11:24-25 TLB; Colossians 3:5; *"He that is greedy of gain troubleth his own house"* Proverbs 15:27; 28:27.

The quality of love for God is also reflected in obedience – John 14:21.

Giving cannot be a substitute for obedience – 1 Samuel 15:22; Proverbs 21:27.

D. Don't _____. *(page 93)*

    1. Panic is always counter-_____. *(page 93)*

    2. What is "terror by night"? (page 94)

        _____

    3. Proverbs 14:30 TLB says, *"A relaxed attitude* _____ *a man's life."* *(page 95)*

    4. When between jobs: *(pages 95-96)*

        What is the best thing to do? _____

        What is the worst thing to do? _____

For Further Study:

We cannot outgive God – *"Give, and it shall be given unto you; good measure, pressed down, and shaken together, and running over, shall men give into your bosom"* Luke 6:38.

Receiving is as important as believing – *"Freely you have received, freely give"* Matthew 10:8; *"What things soever ye desire, when ye pray, believe that ye receive them, and ye shall have them"* Mark 11:24; James 1:21.

Meditate on the Word of God – *"My son, forget not my law; but let thine heart keep my commandments: For length of days, and long life, and peace, shall they add to thee"* Proverbs 3:1-2.

Reject terror – *"Thou shalt not be afraid for the terror by night; nor for the arrow that flieth by day"* Psalm 91:5; *"He shall deliver thee in six troubles: yea, in seven there shall no evil touch thee"* Job 5:19; *"He shall not be afraid of evil tidings: his heart is fixed, trusting in the Lord"* Psalm 112:7; *"Then shalt thou walk in thy way safely, and thy foot shall not stumble. When thou liest down, thou shalt not be afraid: yea, thou shalt lie down, and thy sleep shall be sweet"* Proverbs 3:23-24.

E.   Define "sovereignty." *(pages 96-97)*

_____

1.   What did God do with the bad things that happened to Joseph? *(page 97)*

_____

Read Genesis 50:20

2.   God will work only with what we _____ . *(page 98)*

3.   Define or describe "God's Transcendent Glory." *(page 98)*

_____

_____

_____

For Further Study:

Honoring God results in both giving and obedience – *"Honour the Lord with thy substance, and with the firstfruits of all thine increase: So shall thy barns be filled with plenty, and thy presses shall burst out with new wine"* Proverbs 3:9-10; *"For my thoughts are not your thoughts, neither are your ways my ways, saith the Lord"* Isaiah 55:8; *"Wherefore the Lord God of Israel saith, I said indeed that thy house, and the house of thy father, should walk before me for ever: but now the Lord saith, Be it far from me; for them that honour me I will honour, and they that despise me shall be lightly esteemed"* 1 Samuel 2:30.

Develop a relaxed attitude – *"When thou passest through the waters, I will be with thee; and through the rivers, they shall not overflow thee: when thou walkest through the fire, thou shalt not be burned; neither shall the flame kindle upon thee"* Isaiah 43:2; *"A sound heart is the life of the flesh: but envy the rottenness of the bones"* Proverbs 14:30.

Practical:

In what current situations will you use the following principles?

1. Realize crisis is normal: _____

2. Forgive: _____

3. Admit God is your source: _____

4. Don't panic: _____

5. Admit God is sovereign: _____

Repeat this prayer out loud:

Father, in the Name of Jesus, I release myself from all the things I now see I've done wrong by forgiving myself right now. I ask You to forgive me. And I ask for forgiveness of everyone around me to whom I've been wrong. I accept this new pattern into my life. I love You and thank You for hearing me! Amen.

For Further Study:

God's sovereignty – *"The mighty God, even the Lord, hath spoken, and called the earth from the rising of the sun unto the going down thereof"* Psalm 50:1; *"He ruleth by his power for ever; his eyes behold the nations: let not the rebellious exalt themselves. Selah"* Psalm 66:7; *"Saying, We give thee thanks, O Lord God Almighty, which art, and wast, and art to come; because thou hast taken to thee thy great power, and hast reigned"* Revelation 11:17.

God's transcendent glory – *"And Joseph said unto them, Fear not: for am I in the place of God? But as for you, ye thought evil against me; but God meant it unto good, to bring to pass, as it is this day, to save much people alive"* Genesis 50:19-20.

God cares for His people – *"And we know that all things work together for good to them that love God, to them who are the called according to his purpose"* Romans 8:28.

Self Test *Lesson 5*

1. While in transition, where you are is not as important as _____.

2. Forgiveness _____, unforgiveness _____.

3. Unforgiveness will cause sins to be _____.

4. Men must give utmost attention to their employment and their church, as they are their source.

    ____ True   ____ False

5. Giving releases _____.

6. You cannot compensate by sacrifice _____

    _____.

7. We are normally disappointed in life, not based on what we find, but what we _____.

8. Sleeplessness, fearfulness, mentally searching for answers that don't come, being tempted to quit or

    commit suicide are all obvious signs of _____.

9. What are some right and wrong things to do when you don't have a job?

    _____

    _____

    _____

    _____

10. What did God do with the evil that was meant for Joseph?

    _____

Keep this test for your own records.

Lesson 6

Steps to Entering and Leaving
(Part Two)

Lesson 6
Steps to Entering and Leaving (Part Two)

A.   Don't _____ God. *(page 98)*

    1.   Read aloud: *"Yea, they turned back and tempted God, and limited the Holy One of Israel"* Psalm 78:41.

    2.   God is a _____ God. *(fill in the blank) (page 98)*

       judgmental   harsh   creative

    3.   God is limited in our lives by _____. *(fill in the blank) (page 99)*

       faith   His love   hope

    4.   God puts no limits on _____. _____ puts no limits on God. *(page 100)*

    5.   God can create something out of _____. *(page 100)*

    Read Romans 4:17 and Hebrews 11:3.

For Further Study:

Allow God's creativity to work in you – Psalm 37:4.

God created man with His characteristics – *"And God said, Let us make man in our image, after our likeness; and let them have dominion over the fish of the sea, and over the fowl of the air, and over the cattle, and over all the earth, and over every creeping thing that creepeth upon the earth"* Genesis 1:26.

"For whatsoever is not of faith is sin" Romans 14:23; *"(As it is written, I have made thee a father of many nations,) before him whom he believed, even God, who quickeneth the dead, and calleth those things which be not as though they were"* Romans 4:17; *"Through faith we understand that the worlds were framed by the word of God, so that things which are seen were not made of things which do appear"* Hebrews 11:3.

B.   Humble yourself to _____ God. *(page 103)*

    1.   What two categories of people have difficulty serving God? *(page 103)*

        a. _____

        b. _____

    2.   Humbling precedes _____. *(page 104)*

    3.   Read: *"If you will humble yourselves under the mighty hand of God, in his good time, he will lift you up"* 1 Peter 5:6 TLB.

    4.   With whom does Scripture say God dwells? *(page 104)* _____

    5.   Read Isaiah 57:15.

C.   Trust God to _____ you. *(fill in the blank) (page 105)*

    punish   lord over   vindicate

    1.   Define "vindication."

    _____

For Further Study:

Humble yourself to obey the Word, to bring the blessing – *"All the commandments which I command thee this day shall ye observe to do, that ye may live, and multiply, and go in and possess the land which the Lord sware unto your fathers. And thou shalt remember all the way which the Lord thy God led thee these forty years in the wilderness, to humble thee, and to prove thee, to know what was in thine heart, whether thou wouldest keep his commandments, or no. And he humbled thee, and suffered thee to hunger, and fed thee with manna, which thou knewest not, neither did thy fathers know; that he might make thee know that man doth not live by bread only, but by every word that proceedeth out of the mouth of the Lord doth man live"* Deuteronomy 8:1-3; *"For thus saith the high and lofty One that inhabiteth eternity, whose name is Holy; I dwell in the high and holy place, with him also that is of a contrite and humble spirit, to revive the spirit of the humble, and to revive the heart of the contrite ones"* Isaiah 57:15; *"Humble yourselves therefore under the mighty hand of God, that he may exalt you in due time: Casting all your care upon him; for he careth for you"* 1 Peter 5:6-7.

2. What does Scripture tell you to do if you've been mistreated? *(pages 105-106)*

    _____

    _____

    Read 1 Peter 3:9.

3. Because Jesus held His peace, He: *(circle all that apply) (page 106)*

    a. maintained His power   c. maintained His anointing

    b. lost His dignity   d. lost His self-respect

4. A "root of bitterness" is: *(circle one) (page 106)*

    a. a stronghold of anger and resentment

    b. a bad potato

    c. a feeling of indifference

5. Read: *"Look after each other so that not one of you will fail to find God's best blessings. Watch out that no bitterness takes root among you, for as it springs up it causes deep trouble, hurting many in their spiritual lives"* Hebrews 12:15 TLB.

For Further Study:

Overcome evil with good – *"Recompense to no man evil for evil. Provide things honest in the sight of all men. If it be possible, as much as lieth in you, live peaceably with all men. Dearly beloved, avenge not yourselves, but rather give place unto wrath: for it is written, Vengeance is mine; I will repay, saith the Lord. Therefore if thine enemy hunger, feed him; if he thirst, give him drink: for in so doing thou shalt heap coals of fire on his head. Be not overcome of evil, but overcome evil with good"* Romans 12:17-21; *"Not rendering evil for evil, or railing for railing: but contrariwise blessing; knowing that ye are ... called, that ye should inherit a blessing"* 1 Peter 3:9.
God will take care of those who mistreat you – *"Seeing it is a righteous thing with God to recompense tribulation to them that trouble you"* 2 Thessalonians 1:6.

6. Read Colossians 3:15. What is to rule our hearts? *(page 107)* _____

7. God is your source of: *(circle all that apply)* *(page 107)*

   a. grief   b. wealth   c. worth

D. Write a "T" for True and "F" for False. *(pages 108-112)*

_____ 1. In crisis, one should hold off communicating.

_____ 2. Loneliness and isolation will pervert your thinking.

_____ 3. God can speak to us only through His Word.

_____ 4. The more people who know your troubles, the easier it is.

_____ 5. Good advice is not always godly counsel.

_____ 6. Don't keep your conversation positive; be more realistic about it.

_____ 7. Don't share everything with your children because knowledge brings responsibility.

_____ 8. Tell God only what you think He can handle.

_____ 9. God always builds on the positive.

For Further Study:

Keep your peace – *"He was oppressed, and he was afflicted, yet he opened not his mouth: he is brought as a lamb to the slaughter, and as a sheep before her shearers is dumb, so he openeth not his mouth"* Isaiah 53:7. *"For even hereunto were ye called: because Christ also suffered for us, leaving us an example, that ye should follow his steps: Who did no sin, neither was guile found in his mouth: Who, when he was reviled, reviled not again; when he suffered, he threatened not; but committed himself to him that judgeth righteously"* 1 Peter 2:21-23.
Don't allow a root of bitterness – *"Looking diligently lest any man fail of the grace of God; lest any root of bitterness springing up trouble you, and thereby many be defiled"* Hebrews 12:15.
Peace will guide you – *"And let the peace of God rule in your hearts, to the which also ye are called in one body; and be ye thankful"* Colossians 3:15.

E.   Faith attracts the _____. Fear attracts the _____. *(page 111)*

F.   Act on _____. *(fill in the blank)* *(page 112)*

your feelings   what others say   principle

1.   Whether it be spiritual, marital, financial, social or physical, God begins all healing with His

_____. *(page 113)*

2.   Do you give thanks for the circumstance or in the circumstance? *(page 113)* _____

For Further Study:

God will provide for you – *"But my God shall supply all your need according to his riches in glory by Christ Jesus"* Philippians 4:19; *"But thou shalt remember the Lord thy God: for it is he that giveth thee power to get wealth, that he may establish his covenant which he sware unto thy fathers, as it is this day"* Deuteronomy 8:18.
Keep your conversation positive – *"But let your communication be, Yea, yea; Nay, nay: for whatsoever is more than these cometh of evil"* Matthew 5:37; *"For all the promises of God in him are yea, and in him Amen, unto the glory of God by us"* 2 Corinthians 1:20.
Godly principles are relevant – Numbers 23:19; Psalms 9:7-10; 90:1, 2; 102:24-28; 136; Malachi 3:6, 7; James 1:17.

Practical:

Read Psalm 84:11 and 1 Thessalonians 5:18-19.
How can you implement one of these principles this week?

1. Don't limit God: _____

2. Humble yourself to obey God: _____

3. Trust God to vindicate you: _____

4. Communicate: _____

5. Act on principle: _____

Repeat this prayer out loud:

Father, I may not be in the biggest crisis, yet I know of the times I've been through crisis, I failed in so many ways. Please forgive me for those, cover them with Your forgiveness and love and allow me to live free. I commit myself to act on principle from this day forward. In Jesus' Name, Amen.

For Further Study:

Give praise and thanks to God – *"But thou art holy, O thou that inhabitest the praises of Israel"* Psalm 22:3; *"In every thing give thanks: for this is the will of God in Christ Jesus concerning you"* 1 Thessalonians 5:18.
God always works for your highest good – *"For the Lord God is a sun and shield: the Lord will give grace and glory: no good thing will he withhold from them that walk uprightly"* Psalm 84:11.

Self Test *Lesson 6*

1. God puts no limits on _____. _____ puts no limits on God.

2. What always precedes blessing? _____

3. If we have been dealt with unjustly, we should find a creative way to retaliate.

    ____ True   ____ False

4. **In your own words**, why can a "root of bitterness" be so dangerous to a believer?

    _____

5. What are some dangers of communicating your feelings to the wrong people?

    _____

6. Good advice is the same as godly counsel.

    ____ True   ____ False

7. Whatever you're going through, you should tell everything to your children.

    ____ True   ____ False

8. God never builds on a _____ but always on a _____.

9. We should always act on _____, not emotion.

Keep this test for your own records.

Lesson 7
Mid-Life Crisis

Lesson 7
Mid-Life Crisis

A. Read Luke 16.

1. We are not _____ of anything, only stewards of everything we possess. *(page 116)*

2. List some things for which you will one day give an account to God. *(page 116)*

_____

B. The approach of middle life causes _____. *(page 117)*

1. The result of reflecting back can be _____ or _____. *(page 117)*

2. Only God has the true _____. *(page 117)*

C. Life's greatest wealth is in money. *(page 119)*

_____ True   _____ False

1. What is meant by "funds come from friends"? *(page 119)*

_____

For Further Study:

Faithfulness – *"Moreover it is required in stewards, that a man be found faithful"* 1 Corinthians 4:2.
Faithfulness is the cornerstone of success – *"A faithful man shall abound with blessings"* Proverbs 28:20;
Matthew 24:46, 47.
Adam's job was to steward the earth – Genesis 1:28.
Jesus taught stewardship – *"Then the steward said within himself, What shall I do? for my lord taketh away from me the stewardship: I cannot dig; to beg I am ashamed. I am resolved what to do, that, when I am put out of the stewardship, they may receive me into their houses"* Luke 16:3-4.
Friendship must be cultivated – *"A man that hath friends must show himself friendly"* Proverbs 18:24.
The common bond of friends is their trust – *"A friend loveth at all times"* Proverbs 17:17; *"Faithful are the wounds of a friend"* Proverbs 27:6.

2. Read aloud: *"Never abandon a friend—either yours or your father's. Then you won't need to go to a distant relative for help in your time of need"* Proverbs 27:10 TLB.

3. Distance is never measured by miles, always by _____.
   (fill in the blank) *(page 119)*

   friendliness   physical closeness   affection

4. Life's greatest poverty is not in riches but in _____. *(page 120)*

5. Life's greatest wealth is not in money but in _____. *(page 120)*

D. Failure to prepare is _____ for failure. *(page 120)*

   1. Rephrase Proverbs 22:3 **in your own words.** _____

   _____

   _____

   2. What is the most important preparation of all? *(page 120)* _____

   3. List what, to you, are the most important decisions you'll make in this life. *(pages 120-121)*

   _____

   _____

For Further Study:

If it's difficult to find a friend you can trust, you can still become friends with God and ask Him to find other friends for you – Psalm 16:2, 3, 5. *"Thine own friend, and thy father's friend, forsake not; neither go into thy brother's house in the day of thy calamity: for better is a neighbour that is near than a brother far off"* Proverbs 27:10; *"And I tell you, make friends for yourselves by means of unrighteous mammon (deceitful riches, money, possessions), so that when it fails, they [those you have favored] may receive and welcome you into the everlasting habitations (dwellings)"* Luke 16:9 AMP.

Details make the difference between success and failure – *"A prudent man foreseeth the evil, and hideth himself: but the simple pass on, and are punished"* Proverbs 22:3; *"As the Lord commanded Moses his servant, so did Moses command Joshua, and so did Joshua; he left nothing undone of all that the Lord commanded Moses. So Joshua took all that land"* Joshua 11:15, 16.

E. It's never too late to _____. *(fill in the blank)* *(page 121)*

cry for help   start over   give up

1. Nothing in life is _____. *(page 121)*

2. List some of the things that will change during your life. *(page 121)* _____

_____

3. Explain one meaning of the phrase, "It came to pass." *(page 121)* _____

_____

4. God never starts or ends on a _____. *(page 122)*

Practical:

1. Read: *"Since we consider and look not to the things that are seen but to the things that are unseen; for the things that are visible are temporal (brief and fleeting), but the things that are invisible are deathless and everlasting"* 2 Corinthians 4:18 AMP.

How does this relate to our study?

_____

_____

For Further Study:
God is concerned with detail – Psalm 139:13, 14; Matthew 10:29, 30.
The first step in attending to details is to write them down – Deuteronomy 17:18, 19.
Failure precedes success – 1 Samuel 30:1-20; 2 Samuel 2:4; *"But David found strength in the Lord his God"* 2 Samuel 2:6 NIV.
Pattern for Failure
    Deception: Genesis 3:4, 5
    Distraction: Genesis 3:6
    Dislocation: Genesis 3:7-10
    Destruction: Genesis 3:23
God made everything good, including sex – Genesis 1:31.

2. From this chapter, name some practical ways you can plan for your future, which you can implement immediately.

_____

_____

3. A man named John divorces his wife and abandons his children. Twelve years later he realizes his error and wants to make things right. After several attempts to reconcile with his children and apologize to his ex-wife, John recognizes their deep-seated bitterness toward him. John gives up, believing they are better off without him and it is too late to try to make things right.

In your opinion, is it too late? _____ If not, when is it too late? _____

What can he do now to help his situation? _____

_____

Repeat this prayer out loud:

Father, I thank You, in Jesus' Name, that it is never too late to move forward in You. Your Spirit fills me with creative wisdom. I am well able to conquer, because You dwell within me. Your Spirit guides and keeps me. You go before me, to break in pieces the gates of brass and cut asunder the bars of iron. You make straight the crooked places, so that I may know You and Your riches for my life. I am more than a conqueror through Your love! Amen.

For Further Study:

God desires our highest good – Psalm 37:1-4; Proverbs 23:18; Jeremiah 29:11.
God desires to benefit us – *"He that spared not his own Son, but delivered him up for us all, how shall he not with him also freely give us all things?"* Romans 8:32.

Self Test *Lesson 7*

1. We are not _____ of anything, only stewards of everything we possess.

2. Where do we find life's greatest wealth _____

3. In what way do "funds come from friends"?

   _____

4. Distance is never measured by miles, always by _____.

   friendliness   physical closeness   affection

5. Life's greatest poverty is not in riches but in _____.

   Life's greatest wealth is not in money but in _____.

6. Failure to prepare is _____ for failure.

7. Most of our life will never change.

   ____ True   ____ False

8. It's never too late.

   ____ True   ____ False

Keep this test for your own records.

The Way to Victory

Lesson 8
The Way to Victory

A.   Read aloud: *"Again I say unto you, That if two of you shall agree on earth as touching any thing that they shall ask, it shall be done for them of my Father which is in heaven"* Matthew 18:19.

1.   The place of agreement is the place of _____. *(page 125)*

2.   The place of disagreement is the place of _____. *(page 125)*

3.   What does the tower of Babel symbolize? *(pages 125-126)* _____

_____

Read: *"And the Lord said, Behold, they are one people and they have all one language; and this is only the beginning of what they will do, and now nothing they have imagined they can do will be impossible for them"* Genesis 11:6 AMP.

4.   Powerful breakthroughs come when a family is _____.
(fill in the blank) (page 127)

in agreement   on vacation   well off financially

For Further Study:

God has given us power to overcome any obstacle, enemy or attack through the truth of the patterns and principles in His Word – *"Is not my word like as a fire? Saith the Lord; and like a hammer that breaketh the rock in pieces?"* Jeremiah 23:29; *"For no word from God shall be void of power"* Luke 1:37 ASV.

God's power is released to the degree that obedience is exercised – Revelation 2:26.

God's promises are conditional – *"But if anyone keeps looking steadily into God's law for free men, he will not only remember it but he will do what it says, and God will greatly bless him in everything he does"* James 1:25 TLB.

5. What is the result of parents who are in agreement? *(page 127)*

    _____

B. Define "abiding." *(page 127)* _____

    1. Read John 15:4-10. What does Jesus want us to do? *(page 128)* _____

    2. What gives us strength to endure crisis? *(page 128)* _____

    3. Jesus said to experience Him to be fulfilled in life. *(page 128)* _____ True _____ False

    4. Experiencing a victory during crisis is great, but abiding in Christ continually is _____

        _____. *(fill in the blank)* *(page 128)*

        a lesser victory   no different   greater

For Further Study:

The power of agreement – *"And the whole earth was of one language, and of one speech … they found a plain in the land of Shinar … And they said one to another … Go to, let us build us a city and a tower, whose top may reach unto heaven … And the LORD said, Behold, the people is one, and they have all one language … and now nothing will be restrained from them, which they have imagined to do … let us … confound their language, that they may not understand one another's speech. So the LORD scattered them abroad … Therefore is the name of it called Babel"* Genesis 11:1-9.

Prayer of agreement – *"Verily I say unto you, Whatsoever ye shall bind on earth shall be bound in heaven: and whatsoever ye shall loose on earth shall be loosed in heaven. Again I say unto you, That if two of you shall agree on earth as touching any thing that they shall ask, it shall be done for them of my Father which is in heaven"* Matthew 18:18-19.

5. Read Hebrews 5:12-14 and rephrase **in your own words.** *(page 128)* _____

_____

_____

_____

_____

_____

_____

_____

_____

_____

6. What are spiritual "babes" doing when they continually sin? *(circle one)* *(page 128)*

   a. having a good time   b. failing to abide   c. condemning themselves

7. Read 2 Corinthians 3:18. God wants us to go from glory to glory, not from _____

   to _____. *(page 128)*

8. God wants us to grow up and move from the "milk" of the Word to the_____. *(page 128)*

For Further Study:

Power of agreement – *"And if one prevail against him, two shall withstand him; and a threefold cord is not quickly broken"* Ecclesiastes 4:12.

Abide in Christ – *"Abide in me, and I in you ... I am the vine, ye are the branches: He that abideth in me, and I in him, the same bringeth forth much fruit: for without me ye can do nothing ... If ye abide in me, and my words abide in you, ye shall ask what ye will, and it shall be done unto you. Herein is my Father glorified, that ye bear much fruit; so shall ye be my disciples ... If ye keep my commandments, ye shall abide in my love; even as I have kept my Father's commandments, and abide in his love"* John 15:4-10.

9. We are to search for God's wisdom as if it were _____. *(page 129)*

C. Above the clouds, _____.
   (fill in the blank) *(page 130)*

   are more clouds   the real storm is brewing   the sun is always shining

   1. Write out Proverbs 2:5-6.

      _____

      _____

      _____

   2. Circumstances cannot affect _____. *(page 130)*

   3. God is always working for our _____. *(page 130)*

   4. Read Romans 8:28.

   5. Faith lays hold of truth, and truth always brings _____. *(page 130)*

For Further Study:

Spiritual "babes" – *"For when for the time ye ought to be teachers, ye have need that one teach you again which be the first principles of the oracles of God; and are become such as have need of milk, and not of strong meat. For every one that useth milk is unskilful in the word of righteousness: for he is a babe. But strong meat belongeth to them that are of full age, even those who by reason of use have their senses exercised to discern both good and evil"* Hebrews 5:12-14; *"And I, brethren, could not speak unto you as unto spiritual, but as unto carnal, even as unto babes in Christ. I have fed you with milk, and not with meat: for hitherto ye were not able to bear it, neither yet now are ye able"* 1 Corinthians 3:1-2.
"But we all, with open face beholding as in a glass the glory of the Lord, are changed into the same image from glory to glory, even as by the Spirit of the Lord" 2 Corinthians 3:18.

D. The Bible supports three relationships of God and man. They are: *(page 130)*

1. God is _____.

    God is _____.

    God is _____.

2. Which of these is the greatest revelation to lay hold of? *(page 131)*

    _____

For Further Study:

Wisdom – *"If any of you lack wisdom, let him ask of God, that giveth to all men liberally, and upbraideth not; and it shall be given him"* James 1:5; *"My son, if thou wilt receive my words, and hide my commandments with thee; So that thou incline thine ear unto wisdom, and apply thine heart to understanding; Yea, if thou criest after knowledge, and liftest up thy voice for understanding; If thou seekest her as silver, and searchest for her as for hid treasures; Then shalt thou understand the fear of the LORD, and find the knowledge of God. For the LORD giveth wisdom: out of his mouth cometh knowledge and understanding. He layeth up sound wisdom for the righteous: he is a buckler to them that walk uprightly. He keepeth the paths of judgment, and preserveth the way of his saints. Then shalt thou understand righteousness, and judgment, and equity; yea, every good path"* Proverbs 2:1-9.

Practical:

1. Read: *"[Not in your own strength] for it is God Who is all the while effectually at work in you [energizing and creating in you the power and desire], both to will and to work for His good pleasure and satisfaction and delight"* Philippians 2:13 AMP.

2. If it is true that God is at work within you, to do His good pleasure in your life, what might He be working to accomplish spiritually in your life today?

   _____

   _____

Repeat this prayer out loud:

Lord, I thank You that above the clouds, the sun always shines! I stand in agreement right now with my spouse, prayer partners, pastor and You, that I am one who abides in Jesus Christ! I pray, in faith, right now, recognizing that You are working for my highest good, for Your will to be done in my life. In Jesus' Name, Amen!

For Further Study:

Truth – *"And ye shall know the truth, and the truth shall make you free"* John 8:32.
God with us – *"For it is God which worketh in you both to will and to do of his good pleasure"* Philippians 2:13; *"Behold, a virgin shall be with child, and shall bring forth a son, and they shall call his name Emmanuel, which being interpreted is, God with us"* Matthew 1:23.

Self Test *Lesson 8*

1. What creates powerlessness? _____

2. In the history of the tower of Babel, Scripture records God saying that *"nothing they have imagined they can do will be impossible for them"* Genesis 11:6 AMP. What principle was He referring to?

    _____

3. What is the result of parents being in agreement in the home?

    _____

4. Jesus said, *"If you experience Me, and My experience is in you, you shall ask what you will, and it shall be done for you."*

    _____ True _____ False

5. Which is more powerful? *(circle one)*

    a. having a victory during a crisis   b. abiding in Christ continually

6. We must learn to survive this life, which is from *"crisis to crisis."* _____ True _____ False

7. Some circumstances we find ourselves in can be so severe as to actually affect God's Word.

    _____ True _____ False

8. Faith lays hold of truth, and truth always brings _____.

9. What are the three biblical relationships between God and man?

    a. _____

    b. _____

    c. _____

Keep this test for your own records.

Lesson 9

How to Move from Failure to Success

Lesson 9
How to Move from Failure to Success

A. People may win "victories" but we must learn to _____ them. *(page 135)*

   1. It's easier to obtain than to _____. *(fill in the blank) (page 135)*

       maintain   sell   give away

   2. It is easier to win territory than to _____ the territory. *(page 135)*

B. God's pattern for success is a pattern of _____. *(page 136)*

   1. God never begins or ends on a _____. *(fill in the blank) (page 136)*

       negative   high note   positive

   2. Give an example of this principle. *(page 136)*

      _____

   3. God's plan for us begins with the _____ and will end with the _____. *(page 136)*

For Further Study:

Soft men forfeit victory by seeking to avoid pain – 1 Corinthians 9:25.

Don't compromise with sin. Fight until you have victory. Then you can live in peace – Ephesians 6:13.

God gives wisdom for strategy – Proverbs 3:19; *"Blessed be the Lord my strength, which teacheth my hands to war, and my fingers to fight"* Psalm 144:1; *"Wisdom strengtheneth the wise more than ten mighty men which are in the city"* Ecclesiastes 7:19; Psalms 17:4; 44:5; 2 Corinthians 2:14; James 1:5.

Victory requires a fight – Colossians 1:29; 1 Corinthians 9:25-26.

Victory from strategy brings glory – *"Thine, O Lord, is the greatness, and the power, and the glory, and the victory, and the majesty"* 1 Chronicles 29:11; 2 Chronicles 20:12; *"Be not afraid nor dismayed by reason of this great multitude; for the battle is not yours, but God's ... Set yourselves, stand ye still, and see the salvation of the Lord with you ... fear not, nor be dismayed ... for the Lord will be with you"* 2 Chronicles 20:15-17.

4. How do we get growth in God? *(page 137)*

_____

5. What does it have to do with failure? *(page 137)*

_____

6. What is a "process of purification"? *(page 137)*

_____

C. We must be willing to accept responsibility for failure before we are able to _____

_____. *(page 137)*

1. What happens when we accept responsibility for failure? *(pages 137-138)*

_____

_____

For Further Study:

The Holy Spirit is given to restrain the Christian, so he is kept pure before God in thought, word and deed – *"And I will put my spirit within you, and cause you to walk in my statutes, and ye shall keep my judgments, and do them"* Ezekiel 36:27.

Stay pure – Ephesians 4:17-19, 22-24; 1 Peter 1:14, 22; 1 John 2:15-17; *"Wherewithall shall a young man cleanse his way? By taking heed thereto according to thy word"* Psalm 119:9; John 17:17; *"You are already clean because of the word I have spoken to you"* John 15:3 NIV.

Keep speech pure – *"By long forbearance and calmness of spirit a judge or ruler is persuaded, and soft speech breaks down the most bonelike resistance"* Proverbs 25:15 AMP.

Determine to follow after success and godliness – Deuteronomy 8:18.

Purify your motives and use your ego to achieve great things for God – Mark 12:30.

2. Men generally enjoy going through the testing process a second time. *(page 138)*

____ True   ____ False

3. Why do some people refuse to help with local church opportunities? *(circle one)* *(page 138)*

a. fear of failure   b. too many volunteers already   c. not trained

D.   On what is the fear of failure based? *(page 138)* _____

1. Are humans naturally conditioned to failure or success? *(circle one)* *(page 138)*

a. failure   b. success

2. Read Hebrews 2:14-15.

3. List what is needed to overcome failure. *(page 138)*

_____

For Further Study:

Power to resist wrong is the key to success. Jesus overcame temptation with the Word of God – Luke 4:4, 8, 12. His submission to the Father, resistance to the devil and refusal to sin strengthened His spirit – Luke 4:14. To succeed in life as Jesus did, we must influence people to conform to our godly standard of behavior.

Don't let crises separate you from God. Let God take you through each crisis to the next stage of life – Romans 8:38.

Fear of failure is no reason for lack of commitment – *"For God hath not given us the spirit of fear; but of power, and of love, and of a sound mind"* 2 Timothy 1:7.

Maturity doesn't come with age; it comes with acceptance of responsibility – Acts 13:22.

We cannot mature if we go through life blaming circumstances or other people for our shortcomings – Proverbs 16:2; 21:2; Genesis 3:11, 12.

4. Read Romans 12:2. We must not _____ to this world but be _____ by the renewing of our minds.

5. Read 1 Corinthians 15:45-49. What is our nature? *(page 139)*

_____

6. Read Joshua 1:7-8. **In your own words,** what are the main points about success that God taught Joshua? *(page 140)*

_____

7. God gives instruction in Psalm 1:1-3 for what? *(page 140)*

_____

8. Prosperity is the natural, sequentially-ordered result of what? *(page 140)*

_____

For Further Study:

We alone are responsible for our own life – 2 Corinthians 5:10.

God chastens us – *"But when we are judged, we are chastened of the Lord, that we should not be condemned with the world"* 1 Corinthians 11:32; *"My son, despise not thou the chastening of the Lord, nor faint when thou art rebuked of him: For whom the Lord loveth he chasteneth, and scourgeth every son whom he receiveth. If ye endure chastening, God dealeth with you as with sons; for what son is he whom the father chasteneth not? But if ye be without chastisement, whereof all are partakers, then are ye bastards, and not sons. ... Now no chastening for the present seemeth to be joyous, but grievous: nevertheless afterward it yieldeth the peaceable fruit of righteousness unto them which are exercised thereby"* Hebrews 12:5-8, 11.

Overcome the devil – Hebrews 2:14-15; *"For ye have not received the spirit of bondage again to fear; but ye have received the Spirit of adoption, whereby we cry, Abba, Father"* Romans 8:15.

E. Where does the conversion process take place? *(page 140)* _____

Fill in "T" for True and "F" for False. *(pages 141-142)*

_____ 1. We have no ability to tap into Heaven's resources.

_____ 2. Calvary contains more than salvation; all the resources of Heaven are found there.

_____ 3. God cannot be bothered with our unimportant requests.

_____ 4. Grace, strength, knowledge, wisdom and ability are in short supply in Heaven.

_____ 5. God is a God of abundance.

_____ 6. Jesus is not subject to time or space.

_____ 7. How we feel when we pray determines how God will answer.

_____ 8. God's pattern for success is not based on us but on Christ's limitlessness.

F. Define "emulations." *(page 143)*

_____

Where can you find God's individual pattern for you? *(pages 143-144)* _____

For Further Study:

Identify with Christ – *"For if we have been planted together in the likeness of his death, we shall be also in the likeness of his resurrection"* Romans 6:5; *"So when this corruptible shall have put on incorruption, and this mortal shall have put on immortality, then shall be brought to pass the saying that is written, Death is swallowed up in victory. O death, where is thy sting? O grave, where is thy victory?"* 1 Corinthians 15:54-55; 2 Timothy 1:10.
Renew your mind – *"Do not conform any longer to the pattern of this world, but be transformed by the renewing of your mind"* Romans 12:2 NIV.
The Last Adam – *"The first man Adam was made a living soul; the last Adam was made a quickening spirit. Howbeit that was not first which is spiritual, but that which is natural; and afterward that which is spiritual. The first man is of the earth, earthy: the second man is the Lord from heaven. As is the earthy, such are they also that are earthy: and as is the heavenly, such are they also that are heavenly. And as we have borne the image of the earthy, we shall also bear the image of the heavenly"* 1 Corinthians 15:45-49.

Practical:

1. Throughout this study, we have seen repeatedly that God will not end things on a negative. Why is this so important to understand?

   _____

   Why does this principle need so much repetition for us to understand?

   _____

2. Meditate on Proverbs 24:10.

Repeat this prayer out loud:

Father, thank You that I am more than a conqueror once again today. I turn from the limited, faithless thought patterns I have had and look squarely at all Jesus did for me at Calvary. I am astonished at all You have provided for me through Your Son. Thank You with all of my heart. I trust You to bring me to a new level of living because of this new knowledge of You. In Christ's wonderful Name, I pray. Amen.

For Further Study:

Live the Word – *"Only be thou strong and very courageous, that thou mayest observe to do according to all the law ... turn not from it to the right hand or to the left, that thou mayest prosper whithersoever thou goest. This book of the law shall not depart out of thy mouth; but thou shalt meditate therein day and night ... for then thou shalt make thy way prosperous, and then thou shalt have good success"* Joshua 1:7-8.

Delight in the Lord – *"Blessed is the man that walketh not in the counsel of the ungodly, nor standeth in the way of sinners, nor sitteth in the seat of the scornful. But his delight is in the law of the LORD; and in his law doth he meditate day and night. And he shall be like a tree planted by the rivers of water, that bringeth forth his fruit in his season; his leaf also shall not wither; and whatsoever he doeth shall prosper"* Psalm 1:1-3.

Crucified with Christ – Colossians 1:20; *"Knowing this, that our old man is crucified with him"* Romans 6:6; *"I am crucified with Christ: nevertheless I live; yet not I, but Christ liveth in me"* Galatians 2:20.

Self Test *Lesson 9*

1. It's always easier to obtain than it is to _____.

2. In creation, God began with a positive, but due to the sin of man, it will end on a negative.

    ____ True   ____ False

3. God's purification process frees us from failure through testing.

    ____ True   ____ False

4. Why is it important to personally accept responsibility for our failures?

    _____

    _____

    _____

5. Why are some people afraid to accept responsibilities within the local church?

    _____

6. What is the fear of failure based upon?

    _____

7. What is the natural, sequentially-ordered result of righteous living?

    _____

8. How limited is Christ?

    _____

Keep this test for your own records.

Lesson 10

The Power of Your Confession of Faith
(Part One)

Lesson 10
The Power of Your Confession of Faith (Part One)

A.   Read: *"If anyone publicly acknowledges me as his friend, I will openly acknowledge him as my friend before my Father in heaven. But if anyone publicly denies me, I will openly deny him before my Father in heaven"* Matthew 10:32-33 TLB.

 1.   This principle brings an attitude of _____. *(page 145)*

 2.   The confession of Christ as Lord is the _____

 _____. *(page 145)*

 3.   List types of confessions that help establish the presence of God in our lives. *(page 146)*

 _____

 _____

For Further Study:
Confess Christ before men – *"Whosoever therefore shall be ashamed of me and of my words in this adulterous and sinful generation; of him also shall the Son of man be ashamed, when he cometh in the glory of his Father with the holy angels"* Mark 8:38; *"If we suffer, we shall also reign with him: if we deny him, he also will deny us"* 2 Timothy 2:12; *"He that overcometh, the same shall be clothed in white raiment; and I will not blot out his name out of the book of life, but I will confess his name before my Father, and before his angels"* Revelation 3:5; Matthew 16:17; *"And he saith unto them, But whom say ye that I am? And Peter answereth and saith unto him, Thou art the Christ"* Mark 8:29; Luke 9:20; *"She saith unto him, Yea, Lord: I believe that thou art the Christ, the Son of God, which should come into the world"* John 11:27; Acts 8:37.

B.   Name some effects of praying and confessing the positive. *(page 147)*

_____

_____

1.   Why can't we just pray out all the negative? *(page 147)*

_____

2.   What is a good pattern for prayer for our children? *(pages 147-148)*

_____

_____

_____

3.   How can we release God's power into our lives and those around us? *(page 148)*

_____

4.   Read: *"But what does it say? 'The word is near you; it is in your mouth and in your heart,' that is, the word of faith we are proclaiming: That if you confess with your mouth, 'Jesus is Lord,' and believe in your heart that God raised him from the dead, you will be saved. For it is with your heart that you believe and are justified, and it is with your mouth that you confess and are saved"* Romans 10:8-10 NIV.

For Further Study:

Words of confession and contrition reveal an attitude of repentance and obedience – Psalm 51:3, 4; *"Create in me a new, clean heart, O God, filled with clean thoughts and right desires … make me willing to obey you"* Psalm 51:10, 12 TLB.

Boldness is a form of courage – Proverbs 10:10 AMP, TLB; Hebrews 13:6; 1 Peter 3:15.

Successful men are bold in their identification with their belief, product or activity and in their confession of it – Psalm 119:46; Romans 1:16.

Overcome fear of man, openly identify with Jesus and be bold in confessing Him – *"And fear not them which kill the body, but are not able to kill the soul: but rather fear him which is able to destroy both soul and body in hell … Whosoever therefore shall confess me before men, him will I confess also before my Father which is in heaven"* Matthew 10:28, 32, 33.

C.   Confessing Jesus is necessary to being _____. *(page 148)*

    1.   How do we become acceptable to God? *(circle one) (page 148)*

       a. combing our hair   b. doing good deeds   c. identification with Jesus

    2.   What's the difference between involvement and identification? *(circle one) (pages 148-149)*

       a. One can be "churchianity" while the other is Christianity.

       b. One is more acceptable to God than the other.

       c. One takes less time than the other.

    3.   What happens the moment we confess Christ? *(page 149)*

       a. We are _____ with Him.

       b. He _____ us before the Father.

       c. _____ is pleased with our identification by faith.

       d. He _____ us before men in many ways.

For Further Study:

Identify with Christ – John 12:25-26; Romans 6:4; 12:1-2; 13:14; Ephesians 4:22-24; Colossians 3:1-10; 1 Peter 2:1-3. When we lose our life in identification with Jesus Christ, we find a greater life we otherwise would never have known – *"Whoever finds his [lower] life will lose it [the higher life], and whoever loses his [lower] life on My account will find it [the higher life]"* Matthew 10:39 AMP.

Avoid associations with the insincere "church-wise" who play religious games. Their deception is dangerous to your dedication – *"They will go to church, yes, but they won't really believe anything they hear. Don't be taken in by people like that"* 2 Timothy 3:5 TLB; Psalm 50:16, 17; Proverbs 13:20. *"Wherefore the Lord said ... this people draw near me with their mouth, and with their lips do honour me, but have removed their heart far from me, and their fear toward me is taught by the precept of men"* Isaiah 29:13.

4. How can we see God's results in our lives? *(circle one)* *(page 149)*

   a. pray harder

   b. fast

   c. do what Christ says and confess Him

D. Read 1 Corinthians 2:16.

What is it that we have? *(page 149)* _____

1. What is even greater than us being identified with Christ? *(circle one)* *(page 150)*

   a. God being identified with US!

   b. Being able to get by in this life

   c. Our emotions of joy over it

For Further Study:

Heaven is not reserved for the church-wise; it is the reward of the righteous. Only obedient spirits are allowed into Heaven – *"Who shall ascend into the hill of the Lord? or who shall stand in his holy place? He that hath clean hands, and a pure heart"* Psalm 24:3, 4; Purity is the rule of the day in Heaven – Job 31:1. God looks not at the outward façade of a person but at the heart – *"The Lord seeth not as man seeth; for man looketh on the outward appearance, but the Lord looketh on the heart"* 1 Samuel 16:7; 1 Chronicles 28:9.

Sin is contagious; righteousness is not – Haggai 2:11-14; 1 Corinthians 15:33.

Discipline yourself to do what God tells you to do. Give God your immediate obedience – *"I made haste, and delayed not to keep thy commandments"* Psalm 119:60; Remember that an ounce of obedience is worth a ton of prayer – 1 Samuel 15:22; Psalm 40:6.

2. The _____ establishes God's work in our lives.
   (page 150)

3. What is one true fact of the story of the lepers who did not say "thank you," except for one?
   (page 150)

   _____

4. Confessing Christ is essential to _____.
   (fill in the blank) (page 150)

   knowing who you are in life   commitment to Christ   living a good life

---

For Further Study:

The Mind of Christ – *"For who hath known the mind of the Lord, that he may instruct him? But we have the mind of Christ"* 1 Corinthians 2:16.

"I am the God of thy father, the God of Abraham, the God of Isaac, and the God of Jacob" Exodus 3:6; *"I am the God of Abraham, and the God of Isaac, and the God of Jacob? God is not the God of the dead, but of the living"* Matthew 22:32.

Gratitude of the leper – *"And as he entered into a certain village, there met him ten men that were lepers … And when he saw them, he said unto them, Go show yourselves unto the priests. And … as they went, they were cleansed. And one of them, when he saw that he was healed, turned back, and with a loud voice glorified God … And Jesus answering said, Were there not ten cleansed? but where are the nine? There are not found that returned to give glory to God, save this stranger … thy faith hath made thee whole"* Luke 17:12-19.

Practical:

1. Some people accuse the Church of repressing and suppressing, but Christians actually express and confess. What is the difference?

_____

_____

2. Much has gone awry with the "positive confession" message. What is a balanced view?

_____

_____

_____

Repeat this prayer out loud:

Lord, I want to pray out all the negatives and pray in all the positives. Thank You that You haven't called me to be perfect but to be repentant, and as I repent of all my known sins, I receive Your forgiveness, Your correction, Your grace and Your love in greater measure than ever before. I believe You for the positives to outweigh the negatives in my life and thank You for it right now! In Jesus' Name, Amen.

For Further Study:
"For as he thinketh in his heart, so is he: Eat and drink, saith he to thee; but his heart is not with thee"
Proverbs 23:7.

Self Test *Lesson 10*

1. The confession of Jesus Christ as Lord is the basis of salvation.

   ____ True   ____ False

2. Praise is a positive confession of Christ that charges the atmosphere around us.

   ____ True   ____ False

3. How do we become acceptable to God? *(circle one)*

   a. combing our hair

   b. doing good deeds

   c. confessing Christ

4. What is the difference between involvement and identification? *(circle one)*

   a. one can be "churchianity," while the other is Christianity

   b. one is more acceptable to God than the other

   c. one takes less time than the other

5. The moment we confess Christ, we please God.

   ____ True   ____ False

6. It is far greater for God to be willing to identify with us than for us to be willing to identify with Almighty God.

   ____ True   ____ False

7. The confession of faith in Jesus Christ establishes _____ in our lives.

Keep this test for your own records.

Lesson 11
The Power of Your Confession of Faith
(Part Two)

Lesson 11

The Power of Your Confession of Faith (Part Two)

A.   Fill in the following statements using these words: *(page 150)*

admit   change   confess   believe

1.   We are what we _____.

2.   We are committed to what we _____.

3.   If we don't confess it, we don't have to _____ we believe it.

4.   If we don't admit it, we can _____ our beliefs.

B.   Confession is essential to: *(circle one) (page 151)*

1.   identification

2.   commitment

3.   relationship

4.   all of the above

For Further Study:

God commits to character, not talent – *"Well done, thou good and faithful servant: thou hast been faithful over a few things, I will make thee ruler over many things: enter thou into the joy of thy Lord"* Matthew 25:21; Luke 16:10; 2 Timothy 2:2.

Don't be embarrassed about your commitment to God – Luke 9:26.

Be bold in word and deed – Acts 4:13.

If you make a quality decision to honor God in your thoughts, words, motives and deeds, God will honor you – *"If any man serve me, let him follow me; and where I am, there shall also my servant be: if any man serve me, him will my Father honour"* John 12:26.

Confess Christ – *"Also I say unto you, Whosoever shall confess me before men, him shall the Son of man also confess before the angels of God: But he that denieth me before men shall be denied before the angels of God"* Luke 12:8-9; Philippians 2:11; *"Whosoever shall confess that Jesus is the Son of God, God dwelleth in him, and he in God"* 1 John 4:15; 5:5.

C.   Satan is called _____. *(fill in the blank)* *(page 151)*

the "supporter"   the "accuser of our brethren"   a wimp

1.   What does Satan want for our lives as opposed to what God wants? *(page 151)*

   _____

   _____

2.   What does Jesus offer us to defeat Satan? *(page 151)*

   _____

3.   When we identify with Jesus by confessing Him, we align ourselves with _____.
   (page 151)

4.   It is wrong to say we are: *(circle all that apply)* *(page 152)*

   a.   more than we really are

   b.   Christians

   c.   less than we really are

   d.   growing in faith

For Further Study:

Satan's nature – *"And I heard a loud voice saying in heaven, Now is come salvation, and strength, and the kingdom of our God, and the power of his Christ: for the accuser of our brethren is cast down, which accused them before our God day and night"* Revelation 12:10; Job 1:9-11; 2:4-5; *"And he showed me Joshua the high priest standing before the angel of the LORD, and Satan standing at his right hand to resist him"* Zechariah 3:1; *"Then saith Jesus unto him, Get thee hence, Satan: for it is written, Thou shalt worship the Lord thy God, and him only shalt thou serve"* Matthew 4:10; 16:23; *"Lest Satan should get an advantage of us: for we are not ignorant of his devices"* 2 Corinthians 2:11; 1 Thessalonians 2:18; *"To open their eyes, and to turn them from darkness to light, and from the power of Satan unto God, that they may receive forgiveness of sins"* Acts 26:18; *"And the God of peace shall bruise Satan under your feet shortly. The grace of our Lord Jesus Christ be with you"* Romans 16:20.

5. What happens when we claim to be "less than we are" in Christ? *(circle one)* *(page 152)*

   a. We diminish God's power in our lives.

   b. We are truly humble.

   c. God is pleased with us.

6. Why are many people weak in their faith? *(circle one)* *(page 152)*

   a. They are waiting on God to finish perfecting them.

   b. Their preacher's messages don't teach them enough.

   c. They are weak in their confession and identification with Christ.

D. Write out 2 Corinthians 5:17. _____

_____

_____

For Further Study:

Self image – *"For I say, through the grace given unto me, to every man that is among you, not to think of himself more highly than he ought to think; but to think soberly, according as God hath dealt to every man the measure of faith"* Romans 12:3; *"And these things, brethren, I have in a figure transferred to myself and to Apollos for your sakes; that ye might learn in us not to think of men above that which is written, that no one of you be puffed up for one against another"* 1 Corinthians 4:6.
New in Christ – *"For in Christ Jesus neither circumcision availeth any thing, nor uncircumcision, but a new creature"* Galatians 6:15.

1. How can you exercise yourself spiritually? *(page 155)*

   _____

2. What is meant by "practicing" your faith? *(circle all that apply)* *(pages 154-155)*

   a. rehearsing sermons in the mirror

   b. reviewing your testimony

   c. studying the Word of God

   d. pretending you are a church song leader

   e. confessing Christ privately and to others publicly

   f. memorizing and repeating Scriptures

3. Read Luke 4:1-14. How did Jesus overcome the temptation of the devil? _____

4. Write out Revelation 12:11.

   _____

   _____

For Further Study:

Grace – *"But after that the kindness and love of God our Saviour toward man appeared, Not by works of righteousness which we have done, but according to his mercy he saved us, by the washing of regeneration, and renewing of the Holy Ghost; Which he shed on us abundantly through Jesus Christ our Saviour; That being justified by his grace, we should be made heirs according to the hope of eternal life"* Titus 3:4-7.

Exercise godliness – *"But refuse profane and old wives' fables, and exercise thyself rather unto godliness. For bodily exercise profiteth little: but godliness is profitable unto all things, having promise of the life that now is, and of that which is to come. This is a faithful saying and worthy of all acceptation. For therefore we both labour and suffer reproach, because we trust in the living God, who is the Saviour of all men, specially of those that believe"* 1 Timothy 4:7-10.

Overcome Satan – *"And Jesus answered and said unto him, Get thee behind me, Satan: for it is written, Thou shalt worship the Lord thy God, and him only shalt thou serve"* Luke 4:8; *"And they overcame him (the devil) by the blood of the Lamb, and by the word of their testimony"* Revelation 12:11.

E.   What are some Scriptural truths you can confess over your life? *(page 156)*

_____

_____

_____

Practical:

1.   Lonnie is a man who never rises above the ordinary. He applies for promotions at work but is always passed over. His children are a discipline problem in the school. He feels badly about himself and doesn't admit he's a Christian because he thinks he's a poor example of one.

     What does Lonnie need to do differently?

     _____

     _____

     What can he expect as a result?

     _____

     _____

For Further Study:

Study and do the Word – *"Study to show thyself approved unto God, a workman that needeth not to be ashamed, rightly dividing the word of truth"* 2 Timothy 2:15; Joshua 22:5.

Confess Christ – *"That if thou shalt confess with thy mouth the Lord Jesus, and shalt believe in thine heart that God hath raised him from the dead, thou shalt be saved. For with the heart man believeth unto righteousness; and with the mouth confession is made unto salvation"* Romans 10:9-10.

2. Apostle Paul taught this to Timothy, a young pastor. Underline what you consider are the key phrases in this paragraph:

"Don't waste time arguing over foolish ideas and silly myths and legends. Spend your time and energy in the exercise of keeping spiritually fit. Bodily exercise is all right, but spiritual exercise is much more important and is a tonic for all you do. So exercise yourself spiritually and practice being a better Christian because that will help you not only now in this life, but in the next life too. This is the truth and everyone should accept it" 1 Timothy 4:7-9 TLB.

3. What will you do this week to implement what is discussed in this chapter?

_____

Repeat this prayer out loud:

Thank You, Father, for showing me the truth about the confession of my faith. I want to start confessing the positive, confessing who You are and confessing Your Word. I'm realizing my error and am open and willing for You to start convicting me if I fall back into it again. I want to form a good habit with my words, and I trust You to help me with it. In Christ's Name, I pray, Amen.

For Further Study:

Live for God-given dreams, divinely-inspired desires which are realized through resurrection power within you – *"Work out your own salvation with fear and trembling. For it is God which worketh in you both to will and to do of his good pleasure"* Philippians 2:12, 13.

Determine to live up to the potential that is within you, placed there by God – Philippians 3:12.

Freedom from sin allows God's glory and power to flow through your life – 1 John 3:21, 22.

The Lord's healing, acceptance, power and grace gives the believer the ability to face the world and its reality – Psalm 23:4, 5; Jesus gives a peace, an inner stability, that is a mystery to the world but a comfort to the believer – *"Peace I leave with you, my peace I give unto you: not as the world giveth, give I unto you. Let not your heart be troubled, neither let it be afraid"* John 14:27; Philippians 4:7.

Self Test *Lesson 11*

1. Confession is essential to: *(circle one)*

    a. identification

    b. commitment

    c. relationship

    d. all of the above

2. We are committed to what we confess.

    ____ True   ____ False

3. If we believe it in our hearts, that's all that matters. We don't have to confess it.

    ____ True   ____ False

4. If we believe it, but don't confess it, we can change our beliefs.

    ____ True   ____ False

5. What is one biblical term for Satan? _____

6. When we claim to be less than we are, what is diminished? _____

7. How did Jesus overcome the temptations of the devil? _____

8. Name a few ways we can "practice" our faith?

    _____

    _____

Keep this test for your own records.

Lesson 12

Speaking God's Word

Lesson 12
Speaking God's Word

A. We were created by God to _____ His image. *(page 157)*

    1. As such, we have His _____ power. *(fill in the blank) (page 157)*

        super   creative   lesser

    2. By speaking God's Word, we loose _____ power in our circumstances. *(fill in the blank) (page 157)*

        creative   a little   negative

B. Man is able to influence the outcome of his life with: *(circle one) (page 158)*

    a. repeating chants and poems   b. his words   c. much difficulty

    1. Look up and read aloud Hebrews 11:3.

For Further Study:

As a man, you were created by God to be successful, a hero and a champion – *"And God said, 'Let us make man in our image, after our likeness; and let them have dominion over the fish of the sea, and over the fowl of the air, and over the cattle, and over all the earth, and over every creeping thing that creepeth upon the earth'"* Genesis 1:26; *"For thou hast made him a little lower than the angels, and hast crowned him with glory and honour"* Psalm 8:5; *"For I have created him for my glory"* Isaiah 43:7.

Words are powerful – *"Death and life are in the power of the tongue"* Proverbs 18:21.

Satan wants to destroy our word – Mark 4:15; John 10:10.

We must watch our word – Colossians 4:6; Titus 1:16; James 3:2; *"Keep control of your tongue, and guard your lips from telling lies"* 1 Peter 3:10.

2. Read: *"A man's [moral] self shall be filled with the fruit of his mouth; and with the consequence of his words he must be satisfied [whether good or evil]. Death and life are in the power of the tongue, and they who indulge in it shall eat the fruit of it [for death or life]"* Proverbs 18:20-21 AMP.

   Rewrite the same proverbs **in your own words.** _____

   _____

   _____

   _____

3. All a man's creative force starts with _____. *(fill in the blank) (page 158)*

   a good idea   planning meetings   his word

C. Read Mark 4:39. What did Jesus demonstrate on this earth? *(page 159)*

   _____

   1. Jesus had the Spirit of God _____. *(page 159)*

   2. We have the Spirit of God _____. *(page 159)*

For Further Study:

A man's word and character – Proverbs 21:8; 24:3, 4; *"A good man out of the good treasure of his heart bringeth forth that which is good; and an evil man out of the evil treasure of his heart bringeth forth that which is evil: for of the abundance of the heart his mouth speaketh"* Luke 6:45.
God's Word – Luke 21:33; John 1:1
Our word – Psalm 24:3, 4; Proverbs 25:13, 19
"Through faith we understand that the worlds were framed by the word of God, so that things which are seen were not made of things which do appear" Hebrews 11:3.
Use your words! – *"A man shall be satisfied with good by the fruit of his mouth: and the recompence of a man's hands shall be rendered unto him"* Proverbs 12:14; *"A man shall eat good by the fruit of his mouth: but the soul of the transgressors shall eat violence"* Proverbs 13:2; *"For by thy words thou shalt be justified, and by thy words thou shalt be condemned"* Matthew 12:37.

3. How can we have a greater measure of God's Spirit? *(pages 159-160)* _____

_____

4. Read Mark 11:22-24 and John 14:12.

5. What did Peter understand when he said to the lame man, *"Silver and gold have I none; but such as I have give I thee"* Acts 3:6? *(page 160)* _____

_____

_____

_____

6. Did Paul also understand it? Read Acts 14:9-10.

____ Yes   ____ No

For Further Study:

Use Christ's words – *"And he arose, and rebuked the wind, and said unto the sea, Peace, be still. And the wind ceased, and there was a great calm"* Mark 4:39; *"For he whom God hath sent speaketh the words of God: for God giveth not the Spirit by measure unto him"* John 3:34.

Do Christ's works – *"He that believeth on me, the works that I do shall he do also; and greater works than these shall he do; because I go unto my Father"* John 14:12; *"If ye have faith, and doubt not, ye shall not only do this which is done to the fig tree, but also if ye shall say unto this mountain, Be thou removed, and be thou cast into the sea; it shall be done"* Matthew 21:21; *"Have faith in God. For verily I say unto you, That whosoever shall say unto this mountain, Be thou removed, and be thou cast into the sea; and shall not doubt in his heart, but shall believe that those things which he saith shall come to pass; he shall have whatsoever he saith, Therefore I say unto you, What things soever ye desire, when ye pray, believe that ye receive them, and ye shall have them"* Mark 11:22-24.

D.   Every word we speak is actually a _____ word. *(page 161)*

1.   What are some things we create, good or bad, with our words? *(page 161)*

_____

2.   Jesus said our thought life can ruin us. *(page 161)*   ____ True   ____ False

3.   Read: *"And then he added, 'It is the thought-life that pollutes. For from within, out of men's hearts, come evil thoughts of lust, theft, murder, adultery, wanting what belongs to others, wickedness, deceit, lewdness, envy, slander, pride, and all other folly. All these vile things come from within; they are what pollute you and make you unfit for God'"* Mark 7:20-23 TLB.

E.   Where do your words spring from? *(circle one) (page 162)*

a. your heart   b. your mind   c. outside influences

1.   God's thought life is in His Word. *(page 162)*   ____ True   ____ False

2.   Reading God's Word is often a contest for time or length. *(page 162)*   ____ True   ____ False

3.   Reading the Bible gives you the _____. *(page 162)*

For Further Study:

The creative word – Genesis 1:3; John 1:1-3; *"The same heard Paul speak: who stedfastly beholding him, and perceiving that he had faith to be healed, Said with a loud voice, Stand upright on thy feet. And he leaped and walked"* Acts 14:9-10; *"Verily, verily, I say unto you, He that believeth on me, the works that I do shall he do also; and greater works than these shall he do; because I go unto my Father"* John 14:12.

Watch your heart and words – *"For out of the heart proceed evil thoughts, murders, adulteries, fornications, thefts, false witness, blasphemies"* Matthew 15:19; *"And he said, That which cometh out of the man, that defileth the man. For from within, out of the heart of men, proceed evil thoughts, adulteries, fornications, murders, Thefts, covetousness, wickedness, deceit, lasciviousness, an evil eye, blasphemy, pride, foolishness: All these evil things come from within, and defile the man"* Mark 7:20-23; *"But I say unto you, That every idle word that men shall speak, they shall give account thereof in the day of judgment"* Matthew 12:36.

4. As we begin to think God's thoughts, we will begin to speak God's _____. *(page 162)*

5. Jesus said that the Kingdom of God is "_____." *(page 162)* Read Luke 17:21.

6. What is the best thing you can do when you realize you are speaking a negative situation into existence? *(page 163)*

_____

F. What does "God inhabits the praises of His people" mean? *(page 164)*

_____

1. Speak words of _____, not fear! *(page 165)*

2. To live victoriously, we must: *(page 165)*

   a. Be purified from _____.

   b. Confess _____.

   c. Speak God's _____.

For Further Study:

"*But the fruit of the Spirit is love, joy, peace, longsuffering, gentleness, goodness, faith, Meekness, temperance: against such there is no law*" Galatians 5:22-23.

Renew your mind – "*And be renewed in the spirit of your mind*" Ephesians 4:23; "*Let this mind be in you, which was also in Christ Jesus*" Philippians 2:5; "*Forasmuch then as Christ hath suffered for us in the flesh, arm yourselves likewise with the same mind: for he that hath suffered in the flesh hath ceased from sin*" 1 Peter 4:1.

The Kingdom of God – "*Neither shall they say, Lo here! or, lo there! for, behold, the kingdom of God is within you*" Luke 17:21.

God inhabits our praise – "*But thou art holy, O thou that inhabitest the praises of Israel*" Psalm 22:3.

3. Winners are not those who never _____ but those who never _____. *(page 165)*

Practical:

Read Matthew 12:33-37.
What do you need to do today to ensure your life is built on the right words? _____

_____

Repeat this prayer out loud:

Father, in the Name of Jesus, I see that the worlds were created by Your spoken Word. You have told me to renew my mind and utilize the faith of God and learn to speak to mountains. Please forgive me for wrong speaking that is out of agreement with Your plan for my life. I am called by Your Name, filled with Your Spirit, and my mouth was created to speak in agreement with Your Will. I will use my words to fashion, equip and put in order my life. Thank You for making me a winner in Christ Jesus. Amen.

For Further Study:
The principle of release – *"Then Jesus … breathed on them and said to them, Receive the Holy Spirit!"* John 20:21-22 AMP.
"Either make the tree good, and his fruit good; or else make the tree corrupt, and his fruit corrupt: for the tree is known by his fruit. O generation of vipers, how can ye, being evil, speak good things? for out of the abundance of the heart the mouth speaketh. A good man out of the good treasure of the heart bringeth forth good things: and an evil man out of the evil treasure bringeth forth evil things. But I say unto you, That every idle word that men shall speak, they shall give account thereof in the day of judgment. For by thy words thou shalt be justified, and by thy words thou shalt be condemned" Matthew 12:33-37.

Self Test *Lesson 12*

1. How did the world come into existence?

   _____

2. In Whose image was man created?

   _____

3. God's words contain _____ power.

   Our words contain _____ power.

4. We have the same measure of the Holy Spirit as Jesus did.

   _____ True   _____ False

5. Jesus said our thought life can ruin us.

   _____ True   _____ False

6. God's thought life is in His Word.

   _____ True   _____ False

7. No one can truly get the mind of Christ, even through reading the Word.

   _____ True   _____ False

8. As we begin to think God's thoughts, we will begin to speak God's _____.

9. What are winners? _____

   _____

Keep this test for your own records.

Final Exam

1. Crisis is common to life. _____ True _____ False

2. What are three evidences of faithfulness in a man?

    a. _____

    b. _____

    c. _____

3. Failure can be the _____ of success.

4. God is faithful even when we are _____.

5. What are the five-fold temptations common to crisis?

    a. _____

    b. _____

    c. _____

    d. _____

    e. _____

6. The day before the battle is always more important than the day after. _____ True _____ False

7. If Satan cannot gain an advantage by _____, he will try to defeat by

    _____. If neither of those work, he'll try _____.

8. What is the basic art of communication? _____

9. God's power is released in our lives to the degree of _____.

10. Decisions determine _____.

11. Prayerlessness is often a form of _____.

12. What is one of the strongest weapons we can employ during trials and temptations? _____

13. Your sins and mistakes can take you out of the reach of God's help. _____ True _____ False

14. Forgiveness _____, unforgiveness _____.

15. Unforgiveness will cause sins to be _____.

16. Giving releases _____.

17. You cannot compensate by sacrifice _____.

18. We are normally disappointed in life not based on what we find but what we _____.

19. Sleeplessness, fearfulness, mentally searching for answers that don't come, being tempted to quit or commit suicide, are all obvious signs of _____.

20. God puts no limits on _____. _____ puts no limits on God.

21. What always precedes blessing? _____

22. Whatever you're going through, you should tell everything to your children. _____ True _____ False

23. God never builds on a _____ but always on a _____.

24. We should always act on _____, not emotion.

25. We are not _____ of anything, only stewards of everything we possess.

26. Distance is never measured by miles, always by _____. *(fill in the blank)*

    friendliness   physical closeness   affection

27. Life's greatest poverty is not in riches but in _____.

    Life's greatest wealth is not in money but in _____.

28. Failure to prepare is _____ for failure.

29. What is the result of parents being in agreement in the home? _____

DETACH HERE

30. Some circumstances we find ourselves in can be so severe as to actually affect God's Word.

____ True   ____ False

31. Faith lays hold of truth, and truth always brings _____.

32. What are the three biblical relationships between God and man?

a. _____ .   c. _____ .

b. _____ .

33. It's always easier to obtain than it is to _____ .

34. God's purification process frees us from failure through testing.   ____ True   ____ False

35. What is the fear of failure based upon? _____

36. What is the natural, sequentially-ordered result of righteous living? _____

37. How limited is Christ? _____

38. The confession of Jesus Christ as Lord is the basis of salvation.   ____ True   ____ False

39. How do we become acceptable to God? *(circle one)*

a. combing our hair   b. doing good deeds   c. confessing Christ

40. What is the difference between involvement and identification? *(circle one)*

a. One can be "churchianity," while the other is Christianity.

b. One is more acceptable to God than the other.

c. One takes less time than the other.

41. It is far greater for God to be willing to identify with us than for us to be willing to identify with Almighty God.   ____ True   ____ False

42.   The confession of faith in Jesus Christ establishes _____ in our lives.

43.   Confession is essential to: *(circle one)*

    a. identification   b. commitment   c. relationship   d. all these

44.   What is one biblical term for Satan? _____

45.   When we claim to be less than we are, what is diminished? _____

46.   How did Jesus overcome the temptations of the devil? _____

47.   God's words contain _____ power.

    Our words contain _____ power.

48.   We have the same measure of the Holy Spirit as Jesus did.   ____ True   ____ False

49.   Jesus said our thought life can ruin us.   ____ True   ____ False

50.   God's thought life is in His Word.   ____ True   ____ False

51.   No one can truly get the mind of Christ, even through reading the Word.   ____ True   ____ False

52.   As we begin to think God's thoughts, we will begin to speak God's _____.

Final Exam

NEVER QUIT

53.   Short Essay: "Above the clouds the sun always shines." This simple statement, given in light of all you've learned about crisis, sums up many deeper principles. Write out everything that this statement now means to you.

_____

_____

_____

_____

_____

_____

_____

_____

_____

_____

_____

Name _____

Address _____ City _____ State ____ Zip _____

Telephone a.m. _____ p.m. _____

Email Address _____

The Final Exam is required to be "commissioned."

For more information, contact
Christian Men's Network | P.O. Box 3 | Grapevine, TX 76099
ChristianMensNetwork.com | office@ChristianMensNetwork.com | 817-437-4888

DETACH HERE

Basic Daily Bible Reading

Read Proverbs each morning for wisdom, Psalms each evening for courage. Make copies of this chart and keep it in your Bible to mark off as you read. If you are just starting the habit of Bible reading, be aware that longer translations or paraphrases (such as Amplified and Living) will take longer to read each day. As you start, it is okay to read only one of the chapters in Psalms each night, instead of the many listed. Mark your chart so you'll remember which ones you haven't read.

NOTE: The chronological chart following has the rest of the chapters of Psalms that are not listed here. By using both charts together, you will cover the entire book of Psalms.

Day of Month	Proverbs	Psalms	Day of Month	Proverbs	Psalms
1	1	1, 2, 4, 5, 6	18	18	82, 83, 84, 85
2	2	7, 8, 9	19	19	87, 88, 91, 92
3	3	10, 11, 12, 13, 14, 15	20	20	93, 94, 95, 97
4	4	16, 17, 19, 20	21	21	98, 99, 100, 101, 103
5	5	21, 22, 23	22	22	104, 108
6	6	24, 25, 26, 27	23	23	109, 110, 111
7	7	28, 29, 31, 32	24	24	112, 113, 114, 115, 117
8	8	33, 35	25	25	119:1-56
9	9	36, 37	26	26	119:57-112
10	10	38, 39, 40	27	27	119:113-176
11	11	41, 42, 43, 45, 46	28	28	120, 121, 122, 124, 130,
12	12	47, 48, 49, 50			131, 133, 134
13	13	53, 55, 58, 61, 62	29	29	135, 136, 138
14	14	64, 65, 66, 67	30	30	139, 140, 141, 143
15	15	68, 69	31	31	144, 145, 146, 148, 150
16	16	70, 71, 73			
17	17	75, 76, 77, 81			

Chronological Annual Bible Reading

This schedule follows the events of the Bible chronologically and can be used with any translation or paraphrase of the Bible. Each day has an average of 77 verses of Scripture. If you follow this annually, along with your Daily Bible Reading, by your third year, you will recognize where you are and what is going to happen next. By your fifth year, you will understand the Scriptural background and setting for any reference spoken of in a message or book. At that point, the Word will become more like "meat" to you and less like "milk." Once you understand the basic stories and what happens on the surface, God can reveal to you the layers of meaning beneath. So, make copies of this chart to keep in your Bible and mark off as you read. And start reading—it's the greatest adventure in life!

Some notes:
1. Some modern translations don't have verses numbered (such as The Message), so they cannot be used with this chart. Also, if you are just starting the Bible, be aware that longer translations or paraphrases (such as Amplified and Living) tend to take longer to read each day.
2. The Daily Bible Reading chart covers the Proverbs and the chapters of Psalms that are not listed here. By using both charts together, you will cover the entire books of Psalms and Proverbs along with the rest of the Bible.
3. The chronology of Scripture is obvious in some cases, educated guesswork in others. The placement of Job, for example, is purely conjecture since there is no consensus among Bible scholars as to its date or place. For the most part, however, chronological reading helps the reader, since it places stories that have duplicated information, or prophetic utterances elsewhere in Scripture, within the same reading sequence.

HOW TO READ SCRIPTURE NOTATIONS:
Book chapter: verse. (Mark 15:44 means the book of Mark, chapter 15, verse 44.)
Book chapter; chapter (Mark 15; 16; 17 means the book of Mark, chapters 15, 16, 17.)
Books continue the same until otherwise noted. (2 Kings 22; 23:1-28; Jeremiah 20 means the book of 2 Kings, chapter 22, the book of 2 Kings, chapter 23, verses 1-28; then the book of Jeremiah, chapter 20.)

MAJORING IN MEN®

1	Jan 1	Genesis 1; 2; 3
2	Jan 2	Genesis 4; 5; 6
3	Jan 3	Genesis 7; 8; 9
4	Jan 4	Genesis 10; 11; 12
5	Jan 5	Genesis 13; 14; 15; 16
6	Jan 6	Genesis 17; 18; 19:1-29
7	Jan 7	Genesis 19:30-38; 20; 21
8	Jan 8	Genesis 22; 23; 24:1-31
9	Jan 9	Genesis 24:32-67; 25
10	Jan 10	Genesis 26; 27
11	Jan 11	Genesis 28; 29; 30:1-24
12	Jan 12	Genesis 30:25-43; 31
13	Jan 13	Genesis 32; 33; 34
14	Jan 14	Genesis 35; 36
15	Jan 15	Genesis 37; 38; 39
16	Jan 16	Genesis 40; 41
17	Jan 17	Genesis 42; 43
18	Jan 18	Genesis 44; 45
19	Jan 19	Genesis 46; 47; 48
20	Jan 20	Genesis 49; 50; Exodus 1
21	Jan 21	Exodus 2; 3; 4
22	Jan 22	Exodus 5; 6; 7
23	Jan 23	Exodus 8; 9
24	Jan 24	Exodus 10; 11; 12
25	Jan 25	Exodus 13; 14; 15
26	Jan 26	Exodus 16; 17; 18
27	Jan 27	Exodus 19; 20; 21
28	Jan 28	Exodus 22; 23; 24
29	Jan 29	Exodus 25; 26
30	Jan 30	Exodus 27; 28; 29:1-28
31	Jan 31	Exodus 29:29-46; 30; 31
32	Feb 1	Exodus 32; 33; 34
33	Feb 2	Exodus 35; 36
34	Feb 3	Exodus 37; 38
35	Feb 4	Exodus 39; 40
36	Feb 5	Leviticus 1; 2; 3; 4
37	Feb 6	Leviticus 5; 6; 7
38	Feb 7	Leviticus 8; 9; 10
39	Feb 8	Leviticus 11; 12; 13:1-37
40	Feb 9	Leviticus 13:38-59; 14
41	Feb 10	Leviticus 15; 16
42	Feb 11	Leviticus 17; 18; 19
43	Feb 12	Leviticus 20; 21; 22:1-16
44	Feb 13	Leviticus 22:17-33; 23
45	Feb 14	Leviticus 24; 25
46	Feb 15	Leviticus 26; 27
47	Feb 16	Numbers 1; 2
48	Feb 17	Numbers 3; 4:1-20
49	Feb 18	Numbers 4:21-49; 5; 6
50	Feb 19	Numbers 7
51	Feb 20	Numbers 8; 9; 10
52	Feb 21	Numbers 11; 12; 13
53	Feb 22	Numbers 14; 15
54	Feb 23	Numbers 16; 17
55	Feb 24	Numbers 18; 19; 20
56	Feb 25	Numbers 21; 22
57	Feb 26	Numbers 23; 24; 25
58	Feb 27	Numbers 26; 27
59	Feb 28	Numbers 28; 29; 30
60	Mar 1	Numbers 31; 32:1-27
61	Mar 2	Numbers 32:28-42; 33
62	Mar 3	Numbers 34; 35; 36
63	Mar 4	Deuteronomy 1; 2
64	Mar 5	Deuteronomy 3; 4
65	Mar 6	Deuteronomy 5; 6; 7
66	Mar 7	Deuteronomy 8; 9; 10
67	Mar 8	Deuteronomy 11; 12; 13
68	Mar 9	Deuteronomy 14; 15; 16
69	Mar 10	Deuteronomy 17; 18; 19; 20
70	Mar 11	Deuteronomy 21; 22; 23
71	Mar 12	Deuteronomy 24; 25; 26; 27
72	Mar 13	Deuteronomy 28
73	Mar 14	Deuteronomy 29; 30; 31
74	Mar 15	Deuteronomy 32; 33
75	Mar 16	Deuteronomy 34; Psalm 90; Joshua 1; 2
76	Mar 17	Joshua 3; 4; 5; 6
77	Mar 18	Joshua 7; 8; 9
78	Mar 19	Joshua 10; 11
79	Mar 20	Joshua 12; 13; 14
80	Mar 21	Joshua 15; 16
81	Mar 22	Joshua 17; 18; 19:1-23
82	Mar 23	Joshua 19:24-51; 20; 21
83	Mar 24	Joshua 22; 23; 24
84	Mar 25	Judges 1; 2; 3:1-11
85	Mar 26	Judges 3:12-31; 4; 5
86	Mar 27	Judges 6; 7
87	Mar 28	Judges 8; 9
88	Mar 29	Judges 10; 11; 12
89	Mar 30	Judges 13; 14; 15
90	Mar 31	Judges 16; 17; 18
91	Apr 1	Judges 19; 20
		[You have completed 1/4 of the Bible!]
92	Apr 2	Judges 21; Job 1; 2; 3
93	Apr 3	Job 4; 5; 6
94	Apr 4	Job 7; 8; 9
95	Apr 5	Job 10; 11; 12
96	Apr 6	Job 13; 14; 15
97	Apr 7	Job 16; 17; 18; 19
98	Apr 8	Job 20; 21
99	Apr 9	Job 22; 23; 24
100	Apr 10	Job 25; 26; 27; 28
101	Apr 11	Job 29; 30; 31
102	Apr 12	Job 32; 33; 34
103	Apr 13	Job 35; 36; 37
104	Apr 14	Job 38; 39
105	Apr 15	Job 40; 41; 42
106	Apr 16	Ruth 1; 2; 3
107	Apr 17	Ruth 4; 1 Samuel 1; 2
108	Apr 18	1 Samuel 3; 4; 5; 6
109	Apr 19	1 Samuel 7; 8; 9
110	Apr 20	1 Samuel 10; 11; 12; 13
111	Apr 21	1 Samuel 14; 15
112	Apr 22	1 Samuel 16; 17
113	Apr 23	1 Samuel 18; 19; Psalm 59
114	Apr 24	1 Samuel 20; 21; Psalms 34; 56
115	Apr 25	1 Samuel 22; 23; Psalms 52; 142
116	Apr 26	1 Samuel 24; 25; 1 Chronicles 12:8-18; Psalm 57
117	Apr 27	1 Samuel 26; 27; 28; Psalms 54; 63
118	Apr 28	1 Samuel 29; 30; 31; 1 Chronicles 12:1-7; 12:19-22
119	Apr 29	1 Chronicles 10; 2 Samuel 1; 2
120	Apr 30	2 Samuel 3; 4; 1 Chronicles 11:1-9; 12:23-40
121	May 1	2 Samuel 5; 6; 1 Chronicles 13; 14
122	May 2	2 Samuel 22; 1 Chronicles 15
123	May 3	1 Chronicles 16; Psalm 18
124	May 4	2 Samuel 7; Psalms 96; 105
125	May 5	1 Chronicles 17; 2 Samuel 8; 9; 10
126	May 6	1 Chronicles 18; 19; Psalm 60; 2 Samuel 11
127	May 7	2 Samuel 12; 13; 1 Chronicles 20:1-3; Psalm 51
128	May 8	2 Samuel 14; 15
129	May 9	2 Samuel 16; 17; 18; Psalm 3
130	May 10	2 Samuel 19; 20; 21
131	May 11	2 Samuel 23:8-23
132	May 12	1 Chronicles 20:4-8; 11:10-25; 2 Samuel 23:24-39; 24
133	May 13	1 Chronicles 11:26-47; 21; 22
134	May 14	1 Chronicles 23; 24; Psalm 30
135	May 15	1 Chronicles 25; 26
136	May 16	1 Chronicles 27; 28; 29
137	May 17	1 Kings 1; 2:1-12; 2 Samuel 23:1-7
138	May 18	1 Kings 2:13-46; 3; 2 Chronicles 1:1-13
139	May 19	1 Kings 5; 6; 2 Chronicles 2
140	May 20	1 Kings 7; 2 Chronicles 3; 4
141	May 21	1 Kings 8; 2 Chronicles 5
142	May 22	1 Kings 9; 2 Chronicles 6; 7:1-10
143	May 23	1 Kings 10:1-13; 2 Chronicles 7:11-22; 8; 9:1-12; 1 Kings 4
144	May 24	1 Kings 10:14-29; 2 Chronicles 1:14-17; 9:13-28; Psalms 72; 127
145	May 25	Song of Solomon 1; 2; 3; 4; 5
146	May 26	Song of Solomon 6; 7; 8; 1 Kings 11:1-40
147	May 27	Ecclesiastes 1; 2; 3; 4
148	May 28	Ecclesiastes 5; 6; 7; 8
149	May 29	Ecclesiastes 9; 10; 11; 12; 1 Kings 11:41-43; 2 Chronicles 9:29-31
150	May 30	1 Kings 12; 2 Chronicles 10; 11
151	May 31	1 Kings 13; 14; 2 Chronicles 12
152	June 1	1 Kings 15; 2 Chronicles 13; 14; 15
153	June 2	1 Kings 16; 2 Chronicles 16; 17
154	June 3	1 Kings 17; 18; 19
155	June 4	1 Kings 20; 21
156	June 5	1 Kings 22; 2 Chronicles 18
157	June 6	2 Kings 1; 2; 2 Chronicles 19; 20; 21:1-3
158	June 7	2 Kings 3; 4
159	June 8	2 Kings 5; 6; 7
160	June 9	2 Kings 8; 9; 2 Chronicles 21:4-20
161	June 10	2 Chronicles 22; 23; 2 Kings 10; 11
162	June 11	Joel 1; 2; 3
163	June 12	2 Kings 12; 13; 2 Chronicles 24
164	June 13	2 Kings 14; 2 Chronicles 25; Jonah 1

165	June 14	Jonah 2; 3; 4; Hosea 1; 2; 3; 4
166	June 15	Hosea 5; 6; 7; 8; 9; 10
167	June 16	Hosea 11; 12; 13; 14
168	June 17	2 Kings 15:1-7; 2 Chronicles 26; Amos 1; 2; 3
169	June 18	Amos 4; 5; 6; 7
170	June 19	Amos 8; 9; 2 Kings 15:8-18; Isaiah 1
171	June 20	Isaiah 2; 3; 4; 2 Kings 15:19-38; 2 Chronicles 27
172	June 21	Isaiah 5; 6; Micah 1; 2; 3
173	June 22	Micah 4; 5; 6; 7; 2 Kings 16:1-18
174	June 23	2 Chronicles 28; Isaiah 7; 8
175	June 24	Isaiah 9; 10; 11; 12
176	June 25	Isaiah 13; 14; 15; 16
177	June 26	Isaiah 17; 18; 19; 20; 21
178	June 27	Isaiah 22; 23; 24; 25
179	June 28	Isaiah 26; 27; 28; 29
180	June 29	Isaiah 30; 31; 32; 33
181	June 30	Isaiah 34; 35; 2 Kings 18:1-8; 2 Chronicles 29
182	July 1	2 Chronicles 30; 31; 2 Kings 17; 2 Kings 16:19-20
		[You have completed 1/2 of the Bible!]
183	July 2	2 Kings 18:9-37; 2 Chronicles 32:1-19; Isaiah 36
184	July 3	2 Kings 19; 2 Chronicles 32:20-23; Isaiah 37
185	July 4	2 Kings 20; 21:1-18; 2 Chronicles 32:24-33; Isaiah 38; 39
186	July 5	2 Chronicles 33:1-20; Isaiah 40; 41
187	July 6	Isaiah 42; 43; 44
188	July 7	Isaiah 45; 46; 47; 48
189	July 8	Isaiah 49; 50; 51; 52
190	July 9	Isaiah 53; 54; 55; 56; 57
191	July 10	Isaiah 58; 59; 60; 61; 62
192	July 11	Isaiah 63; 64; 65; 66
193	July 12	2 Kings 21:19-26; 2 Chronicles 33:21-25; 34:1-7; Zephaniah 1; 2; 3
194	July 13	Jeremiah 1; 2; 3
195	July 14	Jeremiah 4; 5
196	July 15	Jeremiah 6; 7; 8
197	July 16	Jeremiah 9; 10; 11
198	July 17	Jeremiah 12; 13; 14; 15
199	July 18	Jeremiah 16; 17; 18; 19
200	July 19	Jeremiah 20; 2 Kings 22; 23:1-28
201	July 20	2 Chronicles 34:8-33; 35:1-19; Nahum 1; 2; 3
202	July 21	2 Kings 23:29-37; 2 Chronicles 35:20-27; 36:1-5; Jeremiah 22:10-17; 26; Habakkuk 1
203	July 22	Habakkuk 2; 3; Jeremiah 46; 47; 2 Kings 24:1-4, 2 Chronicles 36:6-7
204	July 23	Jeremiah 25; 35; 36; 45
205	July 24	Jeremiah 48; 49:1-33
206	July 25	Daniel 1; 2
207	July 26	Jeremiah 22:18-30; 2 Kings 24:5-20; 2 Chronicles 36:8-12; Jeremiah 37:1-2; 52:1-3; 24; 29

208	July 27	Jeremiah 27; 28; 23
209	July 28	Jeremiah 50; 51:1-19
210	July 29	Jeremiah 51:20-64; 49:34-39; 34
211	July 30	Ezekiel 1; 2; 3; 4
212	July 31	Ezekiel 5; 6; 7; 8
213	Aug 1	Ezekiel 9; 10; 11; 12
214	Aug 2	Ezekiel 13, 14, 15, 16:1-34
215	Aug 3	Ezekiel 16:35-63; 17; 18
216	Aug 4	Ezekiel 19; 20
217	Aug 5	Ezekiel 21; 22
218	Aug 6	Ezekiel 23; 2 Kings 25:1; 2 Chronicles 36:13-16; Jeremiah 39:1; 52:4; Ezekiel 24
219	Aug 7	Jeremiah 21; 22:1-9; 32; 30
220	Aug 8	Jeremiah 31; 33; Ezekiel 25
221	Aug 9	Ezekiel 29:1-16; 30; 31; 26
222	Aug 10	Ezekiel 27; 28; Jeremiah 37:3-21
223	Aug 11	Jeremiah 38; 39:2-10; 52:5-30
224	Aug 12	2 Kings 25:2-22; 2 Chronicles 36:17-21; Jeremiah 39:11-18; 40:1-6; Lamentations 1
225	Aug 13	Lamentations 2; 3
226	Aug 14	Lamentations 4; 5; Obadiah; Jeremiah 40:7-16
227	Aug 15	Jeremiah 41; 42; 43; 44; 2 Kings 25:23-26
228	Aug 16	Ezekiel 33:21-33; 34; 35; 36
229	Aug 17	Ezekiel 37; 38; 39
230	Aug 18	Ezekiel 32; 33:1-20; Daniel 3
231	Aug 19	Ezekiel 40; 41
232	Aug 20	Ezekiel 42; 43; 44
233	Aug 21	Ezekiel 45; 46; 47
234	Aug 22	Ezekiel 48; 29:17-21; Daniel 4
235	Aug 23	Jeremiah 52:31-34; 2 Kings 25:27-30; Psalms 44; 74; 79
236	Aug 24	Psalms 80; 86; 89
237	Aug 25	Psalms 102; 106
238	Aug 26	Psalms 123; 137; Daniel 7; 8
239	Aug 27	Daniel 5; 9; 6
240	Aug 28	2 Chronicles 36:22-23; Ezra 1; 2
241	Aug 29	Ezra 3; 4:1-5; Daniel 10; 11
242	Aug 30	Daniel 12; Ezra 4:6-24; 5; 6:1-13; Haggai 1
243	Aug 31	Haggai 2; Zechariah 1; 2; 3
244	Sept 1	Zechariah 4; 5; 6; 7; 8
245	Sept 2	Ezra 6:14-22; Psalm 78
246	Sept 3	Psalms 107; 116; 118
247	Sept 4	Psalms 125; 126; 128; 129; 132; 147
248	Sept 5	Psalm 149; Zechariah 9; 10; 11; 12; 13
249	Sept 6	Zechariah 14; Esther 1; 2; 3
250	Sept 7	Esther 4; 5; 6; 7; 8
251	Sept 8	Esther 9; 10; Ezra 7; 8
252	Sept 9	Ezra 9; 10; Nehemiah 1
253	Sept 10	Nehemiah 2; 3; 4; 5
254	Sept 11	Nehemiah 6; 7
255	Sept 12	Nehemiah 8; 9; 10
256	Sept 13	Nehemiah 11; 12
257	Sept 14	Nehemiah 13; Malachi 1; 2; 3; 4

258	Sept 15	1 Chronicles 1; 2:1-35
259	Sept 16	1 Chronicles 2:36-55; 3; 4
260	Sept 17	1 Chronicles 5; 6:1-41
261	Sept 18	1 Chronicles 6:42-81; 7
262	Sept 19	1 Chronicles 8; 9
263	Sept 20	Matthew 1; 2; 3; 4
264	Sept 21	Matthew 5; 6
265	Sept 22	Matthew 7; 8
266	Sept 23	Matthew 9; 10
267	Sept 24	Matthew 11; 12
268	Sept 25	Matthew 13; 14
269	Sept 26	Matthew 15; 16
270	Sept 27	Matthew 17; 18; 19
271	Sept 28	Matthew 20; 21
272	Sept 29	Matthew 22; 23
273	Sept 30	Matthew 24; 25
		[You have completed 3/4 of the Bible!]
274	Oct 1	Matthew 26; 27; 28
275	Oct 2	Mark 1; 2
276	Oct 3	Mark 3; 4
277	Oct 4	Mark 5; 6
278	Oct 5	Mark 7; 8:1-26
279	Oct 6	Mark 8:27-38; 9
280	Oct 7	Mark 10; 11
281	Oct 8	Mark 12; 13
282	Oct 9	Mark 14
283	Oct 10	Mark 15; 16
284	Oct 11	Luke 1
285	Oct 12	Luke 2; 3
286	Oct 13	Luke 4; 5
287	Oct 14	Luke 6; 7:1-23
288	Oct 15	Luke 7:24-50; 8
289	Oct 16	Luke 9
290	Oct 17	Luke 10; 11
291	Oct 18	Luke 12; 13
292	Oct 19	Luke 14; 15
293	Oct 20	Luke 16; 17
294	Oct 21	Luke 18; 19
295	Oct 22	Luke 20; 21
296	Oct 23	Luke 22
297	Oct 24	Luke 23; 24:1-28
298	Oct 25	Luke 24:29-53; John 1
299	Oct 26	John 2; 3; 4:1-23
300	Oct 27	John 4:24-54; 5; 6:1-7
301	Oct 28	John 6:8-71; 7:1-21
302	Oct 29	John 7:22-53; 8
303	Oct 30	John 9; 10
304	Oct 31	John 11; 12:1-28
305	Nov 1	John 12:29-50; 13; 14
306	Nov 2	John 15; 16; 17
307	Nov 3	John 18; 19:1-24
308	Nov 4	John 19:25-42; 20; 21
309	Nov 5	Acts 1; 2
310	Nov 6	Acts 3; 4
311	Nov 7	Acts 5; 6
312	Nov 8	Acts 7
313	Nov 9	Acts 8; 9
314	Nov 10	Acts 10
315	Nov 11	Acts 11
316	Nov 12	Acts 12; 13

317	Nov 13	Acts 14; 15; Galatians 1
318	Nov 14	Galatians 2; 3; 4
319	Nov 15	Galatians 5; 6; James 1
320	Nov 16	James 2; 3; 4; 5
321	Nov 17	Acts 16; 17
322	Nov 18	Acts 18:1-11;
		1 Thessalonians 1; 2; 3; 4
323	Nov 19	1 Thessalonians 5;
		2 Thessalonians 1; 2; 3
324	Nov 20	Acts 18:12-28; 19:1-22;
		1 Corinthians 1
325	Nov 21	1 Corinthians 2; 3; 4; 5
326	Nov 22	1 Corinthians 6; 7; 8
327	Nov 23	1 Corinthians 9; 10; 11
328	Nov 24	1 Corinthians 12; 13; 14
329	Nov 25	1 Corinthians 15; 16
330	Nov 26	Acts 19:23-41; 20:1;
		2 Corinthians 1; 2
331	Nov 27	2 Corinthians 3; 4; 5
332	Nov 28	2 Corinthians 6; 7; 8; 9
333	Nov 29	2 Corinthians 10; 11; 12
334	Nov 30	2 Corinthians 13; Romans 1; 2
335	Dec 1	Romans 3; 4; 5

336	Dec 2	Romans 6; 7; 8
337	Dec 3	Romans 9; 10; 11
338	Dec 4	Romans 12; 13; 14
339	Dec 5	Romans 15; 16
340	Dec 6	Acts 20:2-38; 21
341	Dec 7	Acts 22; 23
342	Dec 8	Acts 24; 25; 26
343	Dec 9	Acts 27; 28
344	Dec 10	Ephesians 1; 2; 3
345	Dec 11	Ephesians 4; 5; 6
346	Dec 12	Colossians 1; 2; 3
347	Dec 13	Colossians 4; Philippians 1; 2
348	Dec 14	Philippians 3; 4; Philemon
349	Dec 15	1 Timothy 1; 2; 3; 4
350	Dec 16	1 Timothy 5; 6; Titus 1; 2
351	Dec 17	Titus 3; 2 Timothy 1; 2; 3
352	Dec 18	2 Timothy 4; 1 Peter 1; 2
353	Dec 19	1 Peter 3; 4; 5; Jude
354	Dec 20	2 Peter 1; 2; 3; Hebrews 1
355	Dec 21	Hebrews 2; 3; 4; 5
356	Dec 22	Hebrews 6; 7; 8; 9
357	Dec 23	Hebrews 10; 11
358	Dec 24	Hebrews 12; 13; 2 John; 3 John

359	Dec 25	1 John 1; 2; 3; 4
360	Dec 26	1 John 5; Revelation 1; 2
361	Dec 27	Revelation 3; 4; 5; 6
362	Dec 28	Revelation 7; 8; 9; 10; 11
363	Dec 29	Revelation 12; 13; 14; 15
364	Dec 30	Revelation 16; 17; 18; 19
365	Dec 31	Revelation 20; 21; 22

You have completed the entire Bible-Congratulations!

MAJORING IN MEN® CURRICULUM

MANHOOD GROWTH PLAN

Order the corresponding workbook for each book, and study the first four Majoring In Men® Curriculum books in this order:

MAXIMIZED MANHOOD: Realize your need for God in every area of your life and start mending relationships with Christ and your family.

COURAGE: Make peace with your past, learn the power of forgiveness and the value of character. Let yourself be challenged to speak up for Christ to other men.

COMMUNICATION, SEX AND MONEY: Increase your ability to communicate, place the right values on sex and money in relationships, and greatly improve relationships, whether married or single.

STRONG MEN IN TOUGH TIMES: Reframe trials, battles and discouragement in light of Scripture and gain solid footing for business, career, and relational choices in the future.

Choose five of the following books to study next. When you have completed nine books, if you are not in men's group, you can find a Majoring In Men® group near you and become "commissioned" to minister to other men.

DARING: Overcome fear to live a life of daring ambition for Godly pursuits.

SEXUAL INTEGRITY: Recognize the sacredness of the sexual union, overcome mistakes and blunders and commit to righteousness in your sexuality.

UNIQUE WOMAN: Discover what makes a woman tick, from adolescence through maturity, to be able to minister to a spouse's uniqueness at any age.

NEVER QUIT: Take the ten steps for entering or leaving any situation, job, relationship or crisis in life.

REAL MAN: Discover the deepest meaning of Christlikeness and learn to exercise good character in times of stress, success or failure.

POWER OF POTENTIAL: Start making solid business and career choices based on Biblical principles while building core character that affects your entire life.

ABSOLUTE ANSWERS: Adopt practical habits and pursue Biblical solutions to overcome "prodigal problems" and secret sins that hinder both success and satisfaction with life.

TREASURE: Practice Biblical solutions and principles on the job to find treasures such as the satisfaction of exercising integrity and a job well done.

IRRESISTIBLE HUSBAND: Avoid common mistakes that sabotage a relationship and learn simple solutions and good habits to build a marriage that will consistently increase in intensity for decades.

CHURCH GROWTH PLAN
STRONG - SUSTAINABLE - SYNERGISTIC
THREE PRACTICAL PHASES TO A POWERFUL MEN'S MOVEMENT IN YOUR CHURCH

Phase One:

- Pastor disciples key men/men's director using Maximized Manhood system.

- Launch creates momentum among men

- Church becomes more attractive to hold men who visit

- Families grow stronger

- Men increase bond to pastor

Phase Two:

- Men/men's director teach other men within the church

- Increased tithing and giving by men

- Decreased number of families in crisis

- Increased mentoring of teens and children

- Increase of male volunteers

- Faster assimilation for men visitors - clear path for pastor to connect with new men

- Men pray regularly for pastor

Phase Three:

- Men teach other men outside the church and bring them to Christ

- Increased male population and attraction to a visiting man, seeing a place he belongs

- Stronger, better-attended community outreaches

- Men are loyal to and support pastor

This system enables the pastor to successfully train key leaders,

create momentum, build a church that attracts and holds men

who visit, and disciple strong men.

Churches may conduct men's ministry entirely free of charge!

Learn how by calling 817-437-4888.

CONTACT
MAJORING IN MEN® CURRICULUM
817-437-4888
admin@ChristianMensNetwork.com

Christian Men's Network
P.O. Box 3
Grapevine, TX 76099

Great discounts available.

Start your discipleship TODAY!

Call today for group discounts
and coaching opportunities.

FREE DVD!
Send your name and address to:
office@ChristianMensNetwork.com
We'll send you a FREE full-length DVD
with ministry for men.
(Limit one per person.)

ABOUT THE AUTHOR

Edwin Louis Cole mentored hundreds of thousands of people through challenging events and powerful books that have become the most widely-used Christian men's resources in the world. He is known for pithy statements and a confrontational style that demanded social responsibility and family leadership.

After serving as a pastor, evangelist, and Christian television pioneer, and at an age when most men were retiring, he followed his greatest passion—to lead men into Christlikeness, which he called "real manhood."

Ed Cole was a real man through and through. A loving son to earthly parents and the heavenly Father. Devoted husband to the "loveliest lady in the land," Nancy Corbett Cole. Dedicated father to three and, over the years, accepting the role of "father" to thousands. A reader, a thinker, a visionary. A man who made mistakes, learned lessons, then shared the wealth of his wisdom with men around the world. The Christian Men's Network he founded in 1977 is still a vibrant, global ministry. Unquestionably, he was the greatest men's minister of his generation.

Facebook.com/EdwinLouisCole